SCHOLARS BEFORE SCHOOL

*A Complete Preschool Reading Program and Text
For Parents and Teachers to Use With the Very Young*

Joseph C. Johnson, II

Duke University

Illustrations by Lynda Frejlach

Moore Publishing Company
Durham, North Carolina

SCHOLARS BEFORE SCHOOL. Copyright 1971
by Moore Publishing Company, Durham, North
Carolina. All rights reserved. Printed in the United
States of America.
Library of Congress Catalog Card Number 74-140951
ISBN 0-87716-029-5

To all that is beautiful . . . to Elizabeth

ACKNOWLEDGMENTS

The author is grateful to all of the many graduate students over the years for their contributions, especially with respect to methodological descriptions, case studies and trial testing of this material.

He also wishes to thank the typist, Ernestine Webb, whose bright eyes and quick fingers made the longhand scribble rational.

A special note of gratitude is due R. Baird Shuman whose encouragement and penetrating insights were of invaluable measure.

Contents

Introduction

CHAPTER ONE

THE PURPOSE AND FORMAT
The Purpose   3
How to Use This Book   6

CHAPTER TWO

STEP I, EVALUATIONAL SECTION
Format   8
Listening Levels Measure   9
Pre-Reading Stages Inventory   20
Sounding Status Index   42
Social Flexibilities Appraisal   46

CHAPTER THREE

STEP II, GENERIC HISTORY-OBSERVATION SECTION
Introduction   51
GENERIC HISTORY-OBSERVATIONS
One   52
Two   54
Three   56
Four   58
Five   60
Six   62
Seven   64
Eight   66
Nine   68
Ten   69
Completing Your Child's Generic History Form   71

CHAPTER FOUR

STEP III, THE TEACHING APPROACH EMPHASES SECTION

Introduction   80
Teaching Approach Emphasis I, Memory Unit Form   83
Memory Unit Form Exercise Models   86
Teaching Approach Emphasis II, Sound Syntax   97
Sound Syntax Exercise Models   102
Teaching Approach Emphasis III, Visual-Motor-Touch   110
Visual-Motor-Touch Exercise Models   114
Teaching Approach Emphasis IV, Voice-Impress-Look Along,
    Part I   119
Voice Impress-Look Along, Part II   123
Voice Impress-Look Along Activities and Exercises for
    Part I, The Experiences Unit Section   126
Trial Teaching Example   132

CHAPTER FIVE

STEP IV, THE FIRST PHASE READER

Introduction   135
Warmwood and Company   138

CHAPTER SIX

STEP V, THE SECOND PHASE READER

Introduction   261
Questions   266

CHAPTER SEVEN

WHERE TO NOW

Introduction   305
Materials Listing   307
References   310

INTRODUCTION

In a fast-moving and highly competitive age, every parent is concerned with providing for his child the intellectual and technical equipment which will make it easier for him to compete successfully when he enters the world on his own. Over half of a child's education is completed before he enters kindergarten, and his teachers are his parents, grandparents, brothers and sisters, and those with whom he comes into contact in his earliest years.

Obviously, one of the most crucial bits of every child's technical equipment when he goes out into the world — especially into today's world where literacy is a most vital necessity — is his ability to read. No one questions the importance of teaching children to read; many, however, disagree on the question of how early reading instruction should begin. Professor Johnson agrees with those who think that reading can and should be taught as early as possible. He is not alone in his assumptions, and *Scholars Before School* successfully implements them.

Lewis Terman and Melita Oden report that 45% of the children studied in their survey of genius were able to read before they were five years old.[1] Clarence Darrow, the famed "attorney for the damned," reports, "I cannot remember when I learned to read. I seem always to have known how. I am sure that I learned my letters from the red and blue blocks that were always scattered on the floor. . . . It must be that my father gave me little chance to tarry long from one single book to another, for I remember that at a very early age I was told again and again that John Stuart Mill began studying Greek when he was only three years old."[2] Similarly, Norbert Weiner in his autobiography reports that he was brought up in a household in which learning was venerated and that by the age of five he was able to read and "had full liberty to roam in what was the very Catholic and miscellaneous library of my father."[3]

Darrow's contention about his learning letters from his colored blocks coincides with Charlotte Hardy's notion that a child is in the first stages of reading when he shows an interest in letters and in alphabet books and blocks.[4] Hardy also mentions that the child is approaching reading readiness when he pretends to read, and when he asks what a word or sign says.

Much experimentation in the teaching of reading to young children has been performed and its results commented upon. Yale professor Omar K. Moore, using quite exotic equipment, accomplished startling results in teaching very young children to read, and his experiments have been recorded on film.[5] Using a Montessori approach, Nancy M. Rambusch and her colleagues at the Montessori School in Whitby, Connecticut, reported considerable success in teaching reading to children as young as three years of age. Mrs. Rambusch would divide children into two age groups, the three to six, and the five to eight group. Each child would progress at his own rate and would learn reading when it appeared most appropriate for him to do so. Special reading teachers would be available in the first group, and they would work with youngsters on an individual basis.

Probably the most extensive experimentation with the early teaching of reading was conducted in the Denver Public Schools where over 4,000 kindergarten youngsters were involved. The results of this experiment were gratifying merely in terms of the learning which took place. However, four significant guidelines came out of the experiment:

(1) Go at a reasonable pace and limit instruction
to 20 minutes a day.

(2) Be prepared to stop temporarily or to retrench
if necessary.
(3) Excuse from the experiment any child unable
to handle the material.
(4) Avoid pushing the children to get through the
program by a given date.[7]

Certainly the parent trying to teach his child to read at a pre-school age level must bear in mind the guidelines which grew out of the Denver experiment. The child cannot be forced into learning to read before he is ready; many factors, emotional and physical, may stand in the way of his reading, and the over-zealous parent can develop in a child an antipathy toward reading if he forces the child into a pressure situation.

Nevertheless, the child who is able to read early, who is able to distinguish letters by the time he enters school, has a distinct and overall advantage over his peers who are not similarly equipped. Nor should one assume that only the brightest children are able to learn how to read early and are ready to learn during the preschool years. The statistical results of the Denver experiment, while not conclusive, certainly suggest quite strongly that "children of relatively lower intelligence especially benefit from an early start. . . . it might well [be] that slower children need contact with learning to read that is spread out over time."[8]

Surely the encouragement for early reading and the impetus for later success in the structured school situation come from the home. In 1937, Edith Davis indicated quite convincingly that the rate of a child's language development was generally proportionate to the opportunity he had to participate verbally with adults in the family.[9] Generally speaking, the child's early reading ability is directly related to his auditory skills, and ear training such as that provided in *Scholars Before School* has been advocated by a large number of researchers and writers in the field.[10] It is of the utmost importance that children be read to from a very early age, and that they come to hear sounds and be able to differentiate them as early as possible.

In *Scholars Before School*, Professor Johnson has also been intelligently cognizant of some of the visual problems and problems of visual coordination that young children have. He adapts to the purposes of this book the research of such recognized authorities in the field of reading as Frances Ilg and Louise Ames who have observed that three year olds are often able to identify on blocks or in alphabet books the round capital letters such as O, D, C, and G, and the vertical ones such as T and H. He has also carefully considered the fact that the young child finds it difficult to discriminate between b, d, p, and q, and between m, n, h, and u. His examples build calculatedly toward helping the child to develop his ability to discriminate between problem letters and forms, surely the first step toward learning to read.

Scholars Before School is designed for the average interested parent. The book is easy to use, and the rewards involved in using it begin immediately, because the parent or older brother or sister or grandparent becomes directly involved in a learning experience with a young member of the family. Research in reading clearly indicates that it is a rare child who will not benefit from the sort of program proposed by this book.

—R. Baird Shuman, Ph. D.
Department of Education
Duke University

[1] *Genetic Studies of Genius, The Gifted Grows Up*, Volume IV.

[2] *Farmington*, pp. 40-41.

[3] *Ex-Prodigy*, p. 62.

[4] "Prepare Your Child For Reading," *Parent's Magazine*, XXV (June, 1950), p. 36.

[5] *Early Reading and Writing*, 16 mm. film in color, Basic Education Council, Guildford, Connecticut.

[6] *Learning How To Learn: An American Approach to Montessori.*

[7] Kenneth D. Wann, "A Comment on the Denver Experiment," *NEA Journal*, March, 1967, pp. 25-26.

[8] Dolores Durkin, "An Earlier Start in Reading," *The Elementary School Journal*, December, 1952, p. 151.

[9] *The Development of Linguistic Skill in Twins, Singletons with Siblings, and Only Children from Ages Five to Ten Years.*

[10] See, for example, Donald D. Durrell and Helen A. Murphy, "The Auditory Discrimination Factor in Reading Readiness and Reading Disability," *Education,* May, 1953, pp. 556-560; Sylvia R. Gavel, "June Reading Achievements of First-Grade Children," *Journal of Education*, February, 1958, pp. 37-43; and Sister M. Nila, "Foundations of a Successful Reading Program," *Education*, May, 1953, pp. 543-555.

[11] "Developmental Trends in Reading Behavior," *Journal of Genetic Psychology*, June, 1950, pp. 291-311.

Chapter One

THE PURPOSE AND FORMAT

Any adequate program for young children must be adapted to each child's learning style. We cannot expect a three-year-old and a five-year-old child to learn the same amounts of material or to use the same learning modality. Many psychologists tell us that the learning in a child during the first two to three years of life takes place by relying on one sensory mode at a time. Later-learning involves the utilization of many senses simultaneously.

Luria has stated that the degree of cortical development is related to the individual's learned experiences, within genetic limits. This premise implies that the kinds of learning experiences provided early in life will be a significant factor in determining the degree of essential capacities needed throughout the life span. It follows then, that teaching the child to read at an early age can give him a number of learning experiences which will aid him in attaining and refining his genetic potentials.

I mean to stress that many types of reading experiences are

necessary because there is no one *best* way to teach a child to read. According to Durrell, because teachers in various eras have believed completely in only one teaching method, many children have failed to learn to read well. Durrell goes on to say that not only have some educators failed to believe in and to use methods appropriate for each individual child, but they also failed to agree on what the goal of reading is. For example, many of them stated that the goal was to be able to read aloud in a manner pleasing to the ear, pronouncing each word "correctly", and by pausing for all grammatical marks. Others have felt that oral reading was of very little value because comprehension of material was believed to be the ultimate reading goal. And so, these and similar arguments continue, ad nausem. However, it is this writer's premise that if the learning style of the child can be determined, an appropriate method for him can be found and put to use with excellent results.

Before a parent or any other teacher can teach a child to read, he must get to know him by learning his skills in dealing with sounds and symbols, his social flexibility, and his listening or understanding level. This is difficult to do in the typical first grade of a public school, mainly because of the tremendously high pupil-teacher ratio. Therefore a pre-school reading program can be an invaluable asset to the over-all educational program. The need for such a program is being more widely recognized and implemented currently than ever before as demonstrated by the appearance of such federally funded programs as Headstart and Summerthrust programs in which children from culturally disadvantaged backgrounds are being prepared to enter first grade on a level as near equal to their more fortunate contemporaries as is possible.

In these first grade classrooms where one method is not fostered exclusively because there is no belief in an unusual proof-positive method, teachers of reading attempt to make available to themselves as much information as possible concerning each child. The "good" reading teacher usually attempts to do this by trying out sundry tests and teaching methods on various children until he learns for himself what is most effective *for each individual child.*

4

Now mind you, I am speaking here of the "good" reading teacher. Unfortunately, in too many instances, the teacher relies on one standardized reading readiness test or another which predicts who is "ready" to read only 30 percent better than if you or I went into that classroom blindfolded and guessed who was and who wasn't ready for beginning reading.

Generally, according to Adams, Gray, and Reese, "good" beginning reading teachers should ask themselves the following questions before attempting to teach the child to read.

(1) If the child's mental age does not indicate readiness for reading, is there anything I can do about it?

(2) What can I do in the schoolroom to insure the children's health — mental, emotional, and physical?

(3) How shall I plan children's experiences to broaden their general background, thus increasing their understanding and general knowledge?

(4) Can I help them increase their speaking and understanding vocabularies?

(5) How can I help the child to speak correctly?

(6) Are there activities and materials which I can use to develop the ability to see likenesses and differences, to distinguish relationships, and to carry a sequence of ideas in mind?

(7) How can I help children attack simple problems?

(8) How can I use the results of the reading readiness tests to guide in establishing a functional reading readiness and reading program?

(9) How can I set up a readiness program that will provide for varying needs and abilities?

Now we are all aware that some educators believe that the formal teaching of reading is solely the school's business and that, as a consequence, parents and others should not attempt to help their children in this way. In all fairness to those who hold such a belief I must say that in some instances they are correct. We all know that from time to time because of misinformation, belief in an exclusive teaching method, or inappropriate materials some adults have actually hindered their children's progress. However, when you look at the alarming statistics concerning children's reading failure rate in our public schools, numbers ranging with regard to this reading failure rate of from thirty-five to fifty per cent, depending upon the locale and the school, most responsible adults agree that something must be done.

This is what the book you are holding in your hands, then, is all about. It is based on the assumption that something should and can be done. The author is of the opinion that something must and can be done. The author also believes that the good teacher of reading need not be a student of the process for several years nor that he have years and years of teaching experience nor that he be familiar with all of the jargon and technical terminology so rampant in the field.

Therefore, this book is intended for parents with or without teaching experience, older children who are experienced readers, and classroom teachers who want a practical and feasible way to teach beginning reading. The only prerequisite for the meaningful use of this book is that you can *read* it. (For purposes of this book reading is defined simply as the understanding of speech of "talk" in written form. It is, as a little girl once defined it, "Talk writ down.")

How to Use This Book

You will note as you read along in this material that the sections are color-keyed. That is, the parent's or child teacher's, or the classroom teacher's section is *yellow* (no significance should be attached to this color choice) in the evaluational portion, *green* in the general-testing-observation part, and *blue* in the reading approach emphasis section, while the experience unit's portion is *gray*. All other parts are on white paper except the child's and tutor's section which is in *gold and cream*. These sections were color keyed for your convenience since you will need to refer to them on a number of different occasions.

6

As you leaf through this book you will notice that the first section is *yellow* and that it consists of four different pre-reading measures. This portion is used with all children and its purpose is to help you decide what teaching approach you will start with your child. Directions for using this portion may be found on the first page of the *yellow* section. This is *Step I*.

As you continue your brief summary of the material you will discover that *Step II* involves more reading on your part. You need to read this section quite carefully keeping the numbers you learned from the *yellow* portion in mind. Your objective in reading this *green* part is to find the Generic History-Observation that most closely resembles your own child and learning situations.

Once you have identified the Generic History-Observation most nearly like your own situation you are automatically referred to the appropriate part of the *blue* section. There in the Teaching Approach Emphasis part you learn the probable best way to teach your child how to begin reading. This is *Step III*.

After carefully reading through *Step III* you will, at its conclusion, be referred either to the Experience unit section colored *gray* or to the *gold* section called the First Phase Reader. This is *Step IV*. After successfully completing *Step IV* you will be referred to the Second Phase Reader Section colored *cream*. This is *Step V*.

You will have also noted in leafing through the book that allowances have been made if you and your child are not as successful as you may have desired. These allowances are in the form of options or alternate approach emphases to teaching your child. If this occurs, that is, if you do not achieve the progress you feel you should be making, be patient; remember the old saying that Rome was not built in a day; take a deep breath and count to ten, remember that your child is the most precious little human in the galaxy and then try another teaching approach emphasis.

Now that you have learned the major purposes of the book and reviewed its contents go get a tranquilizer, or something, and turn to the Yellow section.

7

You may wish to use this page to make notes concerning points you wish to clarify in regard to the Teach Approach Emphases after reading the following blue section.

Reminder: Be certain to tear out Pre-Reading Stages Inventory, pages 29-39 when you come to it.

Chapter Two

Step I

Evaluational Section

The purpose of this section is to help you get an idea as to the starting point for your child. You will recall that I stated that this portion consists of four inventories. Upon administering these to your child you will have a fair indication of his skills in listening, sounding, social flexibility, and pre-reading stage of development. The rating you derive from each of these four measures will help you identify which Generic History-Observation is most representative of your child. Therefore, it is quite important that you administer them in exactly the same fashion as you are asked.

The plan you are to follow for each inventory is given below.

(1) A description of the measure
(2) Directions for its administration
(3) The inventory itself

(4) Its scoring

(5) The interpretation and use of the score.

The first inventory you will use is the Listening Levels Measure.

DESCRIPTION OF THE LISTENING LEVELS MEASURE

This inventory consists of a series of twelve graded paragraphs in a sequential order of progressing difficulty. This merely means that the selections you read to your child begin at a relatively easy listening level and gradually become more difficult as you move from one paragraph to the next. That is essentially all there is to this inventory.

ADMINISTRATION OF THE LISTENING LEVELS MEASURE

Some morning, before your child has had a chance to tire from the day's activities, ask him to get as comfortable as he can in some easy chair or other and you get comfortable too. When you and he are somewhat relaxed say, "I am going to read some very short stories to you. I want you to sit quietly and listen very carefully to each one because after each short story I am going to ask you some questions which you can answer. Are you ready?"

Wait until your child says he is ready and that he understands what you want him to do. You should reread the directions to the child each time you come to a new paragraph. But, please, reread them only one time for each new selection. (If the child tires after responding to a number of paragraphs, you may stop and begin this at a later time when he is more alert). *If for some reason you deviate from these pre-reading directions the inventory score becomes meaningless and you have wasted both your and your child's time.* So please follow these directions to the letter.

After you have read the first paragraph in a conversational voice to your child say, "Thank you for paying such close attention. I am now going to ask you some questions about the story you have just heard. Listen carefully and answer each question after I ask it."

You should begin with the first question, reading it (and the others) *only one time*, wait for his answers, praise him for his response and go to the next question. The answers your child gives are considered correct only if they are exactly like the answers given to the questions in the inventory.

LISTENING LEVELS MEASURE

Remember, you and the child should be relaxed, read the directions to him and then begin reading.

Date

Score
(Put paragraph letter here)

Write child's answers in the blanks provided.

SHORT STORIES
— m—

Joe saw Kay. Kay was holding a bear.
Joe ran to Kay.

1. Who saw Kay? (Joe)

2. What was Kay holding? (a bear)

3. What did Joe do? (he ran to Kay)

4. Whom do you think the bear belonged to?
   (Kay)

5. Did Kay run to Joe? (No)

Joe and Kay ran down the street. They were late for a party. When they got to the party place, all the other boys and girls were inside. Joe and Kay went inside, too.

1. Where were Joe and Kay going? (to a party)

2. Why were Joe and Kay running? (they were late)

3. How many children were outside the party place? (none)

4. Where were the other boys and girls? (inside)

5. What did Joe and Kay do? (went inside)

Joe and Kay usually go out and play in the morning. Today they went to the playground. It was early, but four of their friends were already there. The boys and girls played *marbles* and took turns on the seesaw. At noon, Joe and Kay went home.

1. Where did Joe and Kay go today? (playground)

2. How many friends were already there? (four)

3. What did the boys and girls play? (marbles and seesaw)

4. What day of the week do you think it was? (Saturday or Sunday)

5. Why do you think the children went home at noon? (lunch)

– p –

Joe jumped out of bed and ran downstairs. It was his birthday. He found a box by his chair at the table. Something was moving in the box. Joe took off the cover and out came a little brown snake. The snake started to crawl and move his tail. The snake was glad to get out.

1. Whose birthday was it? (Joe's)

2. What time of day was it? (morning)

3. Where was the box? (by his chair at the table)

4. What was in the box? (a brown snake)

5. How do you think Joe felt on his birthday? (happy)

– q –

A boy was hurt on our street yesterday. Bill had been playing tennis and was riding his tricycle away from the tennis court when a train came down the tracks. Bill did not see the train coming because he was looking back at his friends who were still playing tennis. The train was going slowly. It hit Bill but did not run over him. Bill was afraid, but only his ear was hurt. His tricycle was badly bent.

1. Who was hurt on the street? (Bill)
2. Why was Bill hurt? (looking back at friends — not watching)
3. What hurt Bill? (train)
4. What game had Bill been playing?   (tennis)
5. What was Bill riding?   (tricycle)

— r —

Joe has an all white dog named Spot. He is called Spot because he has no spots anywhere.

Joe always takes Spot on his trips to the woods. Joe walks slowly, but Spot runs back and forth through the fallen leaves. One day Spot went off by himself. Joe called and whistled, but Spot did not come back. After awhile, Joe heard Spot barking and walked toward the sound. It looked as if Spot had found a little black and white kitten. But it wasn't a kitten, it was a skunk. That night Spot had to sleep outside.

1. What was the dog's name? (Spot)

2. Why did the dog have that name?
   (because he had no spots)

3. What season of the year was it? (fall)

4. What did Spot catch? (skunk)

5. Why did Spot have to sleep outside?
   (he smelled)

—s—

Joe and Kay spend several weeks each summer with their grandparents who live on the moon. Joe and Kay live in a cave, and

13

they always look forward to the summer when they can enjoy the moon way of life for awhile. Joe helps his grandfather with the moon chores. He waters the moon snakes, feeds the moon men, and gathers rocks. Kay helps her grandmother with work in the house and runs errands for her. In their leisure time, Joe and Kay go on long hikes, walk to Mars, or listen to their grandfather tell stories. Grandfather and Grandmother enjoy the yearly visit of their grandchildren. They are sorry when the time comes for them to return to their cave.

1. Where do Joe and Kay go every summer? (moon)

2. Why do they go to the moon every summer? (visit grandparents)

3. What do Joe and Kay do in their free time? (hike, walk, listen)

4. Why do they like the moon? (change from cave life)

5. How do Grandmother and Grandfather feel when Joe and Kay go back to the cave? (sorry)

— t —

Joe and Kay were spending the day at the Fair. They ran ahead of their parents to get to the ticket window. Then they waited impatiently in line to get inside the animal tent. Soon after they found their seats, the spotlight came on. A dog blew his whistle; and the show began. Into the tent center came people riding llamas and horses riding tricycles. There were cows and cats and all kinds of farmers. They also saw frogs that jumped through hoops and monkeys who jumped to and from swinging sticks high in the air. Joe

14

and Kay liked everything they saw; but their favorite was the bear with his fur painted red, green, and black who skipped in and out of the crowd during the entire show.

1. Who took Joe and Kay to the fair? (parents)

2. What was the signal for the show to begin? (dog's whistle)

3. What did Joe and Kay like best in the fair? (bear)

4. What jumped through hoops? (frogs)

5. What did the horses ride? (tricycles)

— u —

Joe and his friend, Sam, had a secret meeting place in a hollow tree at Sam's place. They often met in the evenings or on week-ends and went exploring in the hollow tree. Inside the tree was very dark and cool, so the boys always took along their flashlights and coats. Once, while the boys were playing in the tree, they saw two shiny objects gleaming in a dark corner. They thought they had discovered silver or some precious stones. They began making plans about what they could do with these goodies. Joe wanted to buy a moose, while Sam dreamed of taking a trip to Oz. Finally they decided to examine their find more closely. They moved over to the corner. What they had thought were valuable goodies were really the eyes of Sam's pet lizard glowing in the dark.

1. Where did Joe and Sam meet? (hollow tree)

2. Why did the boys always take their flashlights and coats? (dark and cool in the tree)

3. What did the boys think they saw in the corner? (silver or goodies, or jewels)

4. Who else knew Joe and Sam met at the tree? (no one)

5. What kind of pet does Sam have? (lizard)

— v —

My name is Jose. I live in a suburb of LaPaz, Bolivia. There are ten in my family. My father is a banana picker and my mother works as a helper in an old folk's home. I am 12 and the oldest of eight children, so I care for my brothers and sisters. I have four sisters and three brothers. My youngest sister is a baby only a month and a half old and my oldest brother is 11 years old. On school days I get up at seven in the morning to prepare breakfast for my brothers and sisters, since my mother goes to work very early. After breakfast I help my youngest brothers and sisters to dress and then I take them to my uncle's before I go to school for the day.

1. How many people are in Jose's family? (10)

2. Does Jose have a baby sister or a baby brother? (sister)

3. Where does Jose take his brothers and sisters before he goes to school? (Uncle's)

16

4. Where does Jose's uncle live? (LaPaz, Bolivia)

5. What pleasure does Jose get out of being the oldest? (helps take care of his brothers and sisters)

— *w* —

Rex Labay is the general Manager of a big candy shop in Startex, Alabama. Rex had worked in the store since he was in grade school. He even worked in the afternoons when he was at the University. Now Rex has been promoted to be the manager of the store and that means he tells all of the twelve people who work in the store what jobs to do each day. He has to know how all of the departments in the store operate and he must make sure they work together. Rex has to check the stock of goods in each department to make sure there is enough for the customers who come to buy fresh chocolate, caramel, sugar, and nuts. Another of Rex's duties is to hire workers for the store. After a man or woman has been selected to work in the store Rex has to train the new worker to do his job properly. Rex believes well-trained workers mean more satisfied customers.

1. Where is the candy shop Rex Labay manages? (Startex, Alabama)

2. Where did Rex work while he was in college? (same place)

3. What are some of the things sold in Rex's store? (sugar, nuts, etc.)

4. What do you have to learn to work in Rex's store? (how to keep customers satisfied)

5. Does Rex take orders or give orders?
   (gives orders)

− x −

The Premier of Jupiter is a very important person. When he arrives somewhere, everyone immediately gives him their very best attention. Often a band plays "Hello Holly," a lively waltz, played only to honor the Premier of Jupiter.

He is, in many ways, Jupiter's most important person. His duties are many and varied. For example, the Premier plants a flower every year at the home of the tired Vice Premier. This ceremony expresses the gratitude of Jupiter to a person who is around all of the time. One of the Premier's most important duties is to preside over the football games which make up the international sport of Jupiter. The football players help the Premier make important decisions about what is best for their planet.

1. Name the song that is played to honor the Premier. ("Hello Holly")

2. How does the Premier honor the Vice Premier? (plants a flower at his home)

3. Who helps the Premier decide what is best for the country? (football players)

4. Does the Premier work more or play more? (works more)

5. What is the most difficult duty of the Vice Premier? (to be around)

18

SCORING PROCEDURE FOR THE LISTENING LEVELS MEASURE

Continue reading new paragraphs to the child in the order they are given on the inventory and asking him all of the five questions after each one until he misses four or more of the questions for any given paragraph. When this occurs, stop, tell him that he did a wonderful job and get him out of your hair for awhile by asking him to go play or something.

When you are relatively alone, go over his responses to your questions and give him a score by taking the letter at the top of the last paragraph on which he answered two or more of the questions correctly. Another way of obtaining the same score is to look at the last paragraph you read to him. This is the one on which he missed four or more of the questions and then drop back to the paragraph just before that one and record the letter at its top in the space provided on the front of the inventory.

INTERPRETATION AND USE OF THE LISTENING LEVELS SCORE

Once you have obtained and recorded the Listening Levels Score in the form of a letter, you are ready in the next day or two to administer the Pre-reading Stages Inventory. But in the meantime, you are probably wondering what information the Listening Levels Score indicates.

The Listening Levels Score has a number of implications for the teaching of reading to your child. First of all, studies in the teaching of reading appear to suggest that there is a fairly close relationship between the understanding of spoken words, sentences, paragraphs, and stories and the individual's potential to understand speech in written form, that is, reading. Secondly, other investigations in psychology and reading seem to indicate a fairly high relationship between listening proficiency and the ability to profit from almost all kinds of so-called "book learnings." And thirdly, still other research findings in reading and psychology appear to demonstrate a relatively high relationship between "good listening" achievement and the ability to concentrate on the actual act of reading for any significant period of time.

All of the implications of these findings have been built into this book. So that later, when you have administered the remaining three inventories and have read the Generic-History-Observation section you will be much more likely to have matched your child to the most appropriate beginning reading teaching approach emphasis.

DESCRIPTION OF THE PRE-READING STAGES INVENTORY

Now that you have administered and recorded the score of the Listening Levels Measure and have waited at least until the next day, or longer, if you wished, you are ready to give the Pre-Reading Stages Inventory.

This inventory is made up of five separate parts with each part attempting to get at a different pre-reading stage. The different stages with a brief description of each is given below.

Stage 1 consists of 15 items. Each of the first six items has four geometric designs and each of the remaining nine items has four pictures. In this stage you direct your child to mark the figure or picture that is unlike the others. This stage measures the ability to see differences in geometric figures and pictures.

Stage 2 is made up of 14 picture items. The number of pictures in each item is three. Here you tell your child to mark a specific picture in each item. In doing this you are sampling your child's oral vocabulary, his understanding of concepts, his ability to follow directions, and his knowledge of meaning.

Stage 3 consists of 12 items, each with four letters. This stage measures the child's ability to perceive differences in letter forms. You ask your child to look at the four letters in each item to see which of the four is not the same as the other three.

Stage 4 is a matching stage consisting of 12 items with two letters each. Here your child is asked to match letters in the first column with corresponding letters in the second column. This stage measures ability to discern similarities in letter forms.

Stage 5 is comprised of 21 items with five letters or words in each. Your child should be able to recognize the key letter or word symbol on the left among the four alternatives given to the right of the line. This stage measures his skill in recognizing similarities and differences in letter and word formations from the most simple type of large differences to complex and minute changes.

ADMINISTRATION OF THE PRE-READING STAGES INVENTORY

Again, as with the Listening Levels Measure, you are asked to follow the directions for administration to the letter. During the administration of this inventory, it is important that you are comfortable, have practiced giving it in your mind, and have placed your child at a comfortable writing table where he can reach the book without stretching and where he has plenty of elbow room. In addition, you will have made certain that Sam or Kay is not tired and is ready and wants to play this game with you.

Materials you will need to give this inventory include a clock or watch with a sweep second hand, this book, of course, and two or more large pencils or crayons (sometimes these latter items have a way of accidentally breaking themselves). Of these items just mentioned, the clock or watch with a sweep second hand is very important. The reason for saying this is that the different stages are timed . . . and if you do not time them exactly as the directions say, the scores will not be worth anything. So you will have just wasted you and your child's time and also have lost a source of valuable information.

This inventory takes no more than 14 minutes of child marking time. Remember the directions must be given carefully. Be sure that your child understands them. You may help him on the practice items. Be certain that he has marked each practice item correctly. If desired, practice items for Stages 1 and 4 may be duplicated on another piece of paper by you. You may stop at the completion of any stage and give your child a 10 or 15 minute break, or longer if necessary. However, you should complete the inventory by the end of two consecutive mornings at the most. You are now ready to administer the inventory.

INTRODUCTION

Say: "We are going to play a new game today. You will have to listen very carefully because I will tell you what to do just once. I am going to put this paper on your table. (Tear out inventory.) Do not open it until I tell you." (Place the inventory face-up in front of him.)

Stage I (4 minutes total child marking time)

Say: "You can have no help in playing this game. You must play by yourself. Open the first page and turn back like this." (Help him. Be sure your child has the right place.)

Say: "On this page are some pictures with different shapes. Look at the pictures. Can you find the one that is not the same as the others? (Have your child answer.) Yes, it is this one. (Point to the correct one.) Now draw a line through it to show that it does not belong there. Do it now."

(Inspect your child's work. See that he has done the practice item correctly. Help him if necessary).

Say: "Find the picture in this row that is not the same as the others and draw a line through it." (the rectangle)

Say: "Start here. (Point to row 1.) Find the picture in each row that is not the same as the others. Draw a line through it. Do all of them on this page. Ready, begin."

At the end of 2 minutes say "Stop."

Say: "Turn to the second page and fold it back." (Help him.)

(Be sure he has the correct page.)

Say: "Draw a line through the picture on each row that is not the same as the others. Begin with the row of cats (Row 7) and then the rest of the rows."

At the end of 2 minutes say "Stop."

Stage 2 (2 minutes child marking time)

Turn to the next page and fold it back. (Help him.)

(Be sure he has the correct page.)

Say: "Now find the ice cream cones and the piece of pie." (Assist him in finding the item.)

Say: "Listen carefully and do just what I say. Put a mark on the piece of pie."

(See that he has marked the pie. If necessary illustrate on a separate sheet of paper.)

Say: "Now go to the next row. Put a mark on the animal that has the longest tail."

(See that he has marked the cat.   Help him in finding this and all other items of stage 2. Allow about five seconds for him to answer.)

Say: "Now go to the next row. (No. 1) Put a mark on the boy with one leg."

(Allow about 5 seconds for each answer.)

Say: "Now go to the next row. Put a mark on the smallest tree."

Say: "Now go to the next row. Put a mark on the knife.
Put a mark on the thing you can wear.
Now turn your paper over and fold it back. (Turn to the next page.)
Find the mice." (Help him.)

Say: "Put a mark on the mouse that is upside down.
Now go to the next row. (No. 6) Put a mark on the saddest face."

Say: "Now go to the next row. Put a mark on the shortest crayon.
Now move to the next row. Put a mark on the animal that has no ears.
Now, put a mark on the head with the most hair. (No. 9)
Now turn your paper over. Find the three cups." (Row 10, next page)

Say: "Put a mark on the cup at the end.

Say: Now move on and put a mark on the tallest lamp.
        Now move down and put a mark on the pencil in the middle.
        Now put a mark on the first tree.
        Put a mark on the mouse that is not following the other mouse.
        Now turn your paper over."

Stage 3 (1 minute total marking time)

Say: "Look at the first row of letters. (Point to RRXR). Can you find the letter that is not the same as the other letters? (Wait for him to answer). Yes. Now draw a line through it to show that it does not belong there." (Demonstrate by drawing a line through the X).

        (Look at his work. Lines should be heavily drawn so that they are easily visible. Help him draw lines through the letters if necessary.)

Say: "Now move down one row. (Help him if necessary). Find the letter in this row that is not the same as the other letters and draw a line through it." (Demonstrate by drawing a line through the T).

        (Using these same directions, have him draw a line through W and Y in the next two rows. Be sure he is doing the practice items correctly. Do not help him in marking after the practice items.)

Say: "Start here. (Point to the XXUX, row 1.) Find the letter in each row that is not the same as the other letters and draw a line through it. Do all of them on this page. Ready, begin."

Say: "Turn to the next page and fold it back." (Show him.)

Say: "On this page are some letters. Look at the first large letter. (Point to the P.) Can you find a letter here (Point down the right column.) that looks exactly like this one? (Have him answer). Yes, it is this one. (Point to the P on the right). Pick up your pencil now, and draw a line from this letter to this one. (Point and draw while giving directions.) Do it now. Make your line touch the letters."

(Inspect his work. See that your child has done the practice item correctly. Help him draw the lines if necessary.)

Say: "Now look at this letter. (Point to the L.) Find the letter that looks exactly like it and draw a line from this letter to this one."

Use the same directions for practice items C and D. Inspect the child's work and assist him if necessary.

Say: "I want you to do all the rest of the letters on the page in the same way. (Be sure he has the correct place.) Ready? Begin."

Say: "Turn to the next page and fold it back like this." (Show him.)

Stage 5

(You do not need to time this last test very closely.

You may allow him up to 5 minutes to do it.)

Say: "Now find the first row of letters. Look at the first letter and then find another which is just like it. Draw a circle around it."

(Assist him in marking the circle around the letter A to the right of the dotted vertical line.)

Say: "In each row you will find something on this side of the dotted line. (Demonstrate by pointing to the items.) You must then find something on the other side of the dotted line just like it."

Say: "Now find a letter which is just like the first letter. Put a circle around it. (Allow about 15 seconds.)
Now do the next one in the same way (allow about 15 seconds.)
Now do all the rest of the page."

(Encourage him to do the other exercises on this page. In order to permit every pupil to try to do all that he can this last stage is not strictly timed. When he has completed the page or done all he is able to, turn to the next page.)

Say: "Now turn the page over. (Pause.) Here are more words. Find the word or words which are just like the first word or words. Put a mark on it. (pause.)
Do all of these the same way."

(When he has completed the page, or has done all he seems able to do, take the inventory.)

Maximum time allotment for entire inventory is no more than 14 minutes.

Now that you have examined the directions for the administration of this inventory, look closely at the inventory itself after first tearing it out of this book. Be careful that you tear out only those pages that have been perforated and then put them together with a paper clip.

Once you have removed these pages, study them carefully by looking at each page while re-reading the directions for the inventory administration.

Name   Date

                    Number Correct   Converted Scores
                                              (from the score scale)

Stage 1

Stage 2

Stage 3

Stage 4

Stage 5

Pre Reading Stages Inventory

Stage I

Practice Items

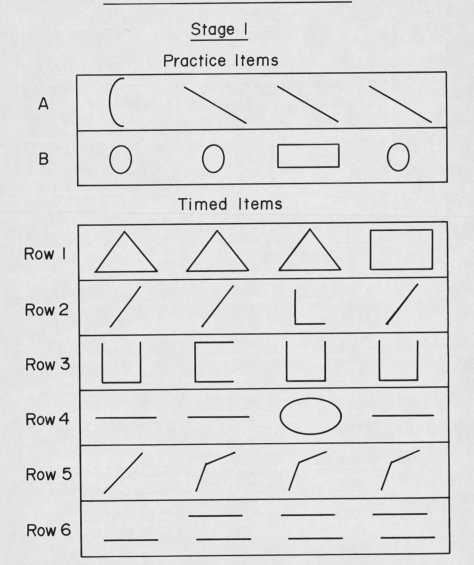

29

Row 7

Row 8

Row 9

Row 10

Row 11

Row 12

Row 13

Row 14

Row 15

Stage 2

Practice Items

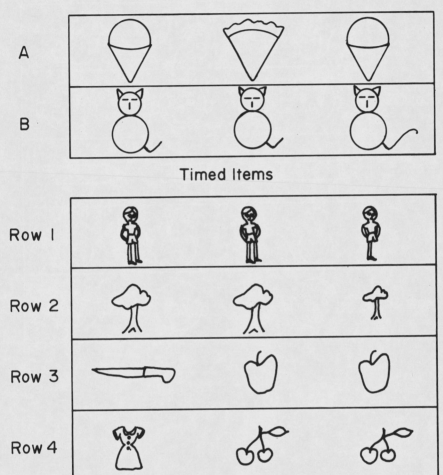

Timed Items

Row 1

Row 2

Row 3

Row 4

Row 5

Row 6

Row 7

Row 8

Row 9

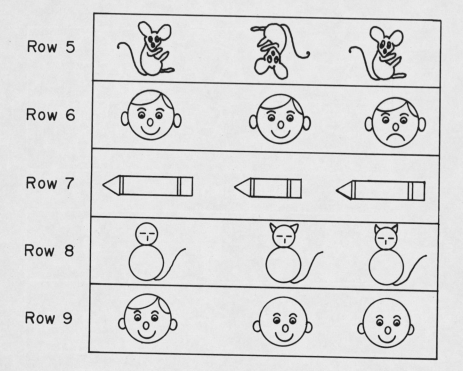

Stage 2 , continued

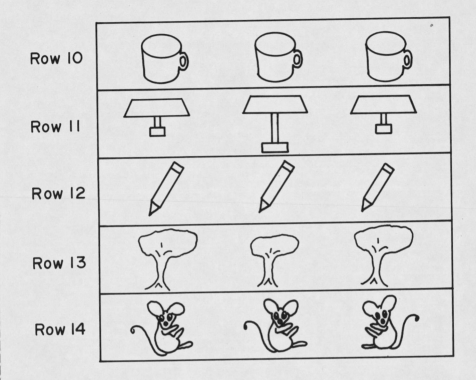

Row 10

Row 11

Row 12

Row 13

Row 14

Stage 3

Practice Items

R R X R

V V V T

S S W S

Y Z Z Z

Timed Items

Row 1   X X U X

Row 2   B C B B

Row 3   D D E D

Row 4   P d P P

Row 5   V V V W

Row 6   M N M M

Row 7   d b b b

Row 8   J P J J

Row 9   A A Y A

Row 10   O P P P

Row 11   f f t f

Row 12   O O G O

Stage 4

Practice Items

P D

L L

C P

D C

Timed Items

X O

M N

O X

N M

a b

c e

e c

b a

s g

r s

g r

p p

Stage 5

Practice Item

| T | D | A | V | | A |

Timed Items

R	C	O	P		R
W	T	S	X		X
d	b	p	o		d

no	on	as	no	if
it	at	it	go	is
so	of	so	at	an
come	said	hope	come	hair
here	were	call	ball	here
side	hide	side	lied	bide
horse	course	remorse	alone	horse

Stage 5

continued

sing   ring   bring   bright

drive   alive   drip   dice

to say   to be   to see   to me

and them   and so   and those   and then

I am   I saw   I was   I ran

bring

drive

to be

and then

I was

you are	yard you are you were yipes
all right	all red all ripe all right already
he was not	he was not she was not it was not he was so
I am good.	I am bad. I am good. I am green. I am great
no, not yet	no, not wet no, not fat no, not yes no, not yet
who are you?	who are they? who were they? who are you?

SCORING PROCEDURE FOR THE PRE-READING STAGES INVENTORY

When your child has finished taking the inventory, praise him for the tremendous job he has done, and then you and he separate for awhile. When this has been accomplished and you feel like it, you can score the inventory. Do this by going over the inventory with the directions for its administration, counting at each of the five stages those items he got correct. After determining the number of correct items for each stage, record these numbers in the space provided on the first page of the inventory under the heading of child's score.

Then take your child's score for each of the five stages to the scale below, find his converted score for each stage and put these numbers in the appropriate blanks on the first page of this inventory. For instance, if your child got a total score in Stage 1 of seven, his converted score would be 2a. Say, in Stage 2 his score was nine for a converted score of 2b, in Stage 3 he got four right for a converted score of 2c, while in Stage 4 he made ten right for a converted score of 3d, and finally, in Stage five he had 2 correct responses for a converted score of 1e. His entire Pre-reading Stages Inventory then would read 2a, 2b, 2c, 3d, 1e.

PRE-READING STAGES INVENTORY CONVERTED SCORE SCALE

Stage 1	Number Correct	Converted Score
Stage 1	8 to 15	3a
	4 to 7	2a
	3 or less	1a
Stage 2	10 to 14	3b
	4 to 9	2b
	3 or less	1b
Stage 3	8 to 12	3c
	4 to 7	2c
	3 or less	1c

	Number Correct	Converted Score
	8 to 12	3d
Stage 4	4 to 7	2d
	3 or less	1d
	10 to 21	3e
Stage 5	4 to 9	2e
	3 or less	1e

Now that you have derived the converted score by using the preceding scale you have only one remaining inventory to give your child directly. But in the meantime let us look more closely at the Pre-Reading Stages Inventory.

INTERPRETATION AND USE OF THE PRE-READING INVENTORY

After you have listed the Pre-Reading Stages Inventory score in the form of a five letter and five number combination, what do you really have? You will recall that the inventory is divided into five parts or stages. They are in the order you administered them: (1) visual discrimination, (2) vocabulary and following instructions, (3) letter symbols cross out; (4) letter symbols matching, and (5) identification of symbols and units.

Let us examine each one of these in turn. The first stage, visual discrimination, gives you some idea of how well and to what degree your child can tell differences among written symbols and pictures. Studies indicate that this is a skill basic to all kinds of reading. Stage 2 tells us how well your child follows oral directions and gives us an idea of his understanding and command of oral language needed for everyday life. Investigations in the field of reading appear to tell us that in order to profit from reading instruction the child must be able to follow simple oral directions and he must have a speaking knowledge of a variety of words with which to express ideas about his life and environment. Stages 3 and 4 are concerned with the child's ability to see differences and similarities among letters. These are necessary skills for the child to have before he can ever read. Stage 5 deals with the actual reading of letters and words in that he must say them mentally in order to get them correct. If your child got most of these correct, he will probably be reading from the First Phase Reader in the last part of the book in a matter of days. If he didn't know them, take heart; it will probably just take a little longer.

The appropriate use of the information you obtained on the Pre-Reading Stages Inventory will be made prior to the time you begin teaching your child to actually read. This time will arrive after you give your child the Sounding Status Index, complete the Social Flexibilities Appraisal, and read the Generic History-Observations. Then you will be able to apply this information toward the selection of the most appropriate teaching approach for him.

DESCRIPTION OF THE SOUNDING STATUS INDEX

This is the last inventory you will administer directly to your child. The Sounding Status Index is designed to give you information with respect to your child's skill in hearing differences among spoken speech sounds. It is comprised of five parts and is very simple to administer.

The plan and procedure for administering the Index are somewhat different from the administration of the first two inventories in that the Index provides directions for administering and scoring in the same section. After both you and your child are comfortable in some easy chair, tell him you would like to play some word games with him for the next few minutes. (It will take about nine or ten minutes to administer the Index.) Look over the Index yourself for a couple of minutes and then administer it.

THE SOUNDING STATUS INDEX AND ITS ADMINISTRATION
AND SCORING
Sounding Status Index

Name ————————————— Date —————————

Total score ———————— (number correct) ————

Part I

Show your child the following five rows of words and ask him to tell you those which sound like the key word. Tell him what the key word is. (This is the word to the left of the black bar). Point to and name each word in turn, in each row after the double bar. You make a mark on those he correctly identifies. Allow about five seconds for him to respond to any one word, then go to the next one.

Pan		Fan	Cat	Man
Lock		Rock	Sock	Bug
Dot		Bridge	Pot	Cot
Bat		Cat	Hat	Clock
Head		Bed	Fire	Shed

Write the number correct here.

Part II

Ask your child to listen very carefully to each word you say because after each one you want him to tell you a word that sounds like or rhymes with it. Say: "If I said rat, you might say mat because that is a word that sounds like (or rhymes) with rat. OK. Now my word is *Ted*. What word can you say that sounds like it." Repeat these directions if necessary for each word you give him. Use the following words: money, far, mouse, most, and mud.

Allow about five seconds for him to give you a word. Count any word right that is a real word and that rhymes. Give him only one chance at each word. Write the number correct here.

Part III

Again ask your child to listen very carefully to every word you are about to say because after each one you want him to give you a word which begins with the same sound. Do not stress the beginning sound. Allow about five seconds for him to respond. Give him only one chance for each word.

Say: "If I said move, what word could you give me that begins with that same sound? O.K. Since I said move, you could have said mother or Mary or maybe monster. These words all begin with the same sound."

Present the following words to your child without emphasizing the beginning sound and if he gives you rhyming words that do not begin with the appropriate letter sound go back and give him directions again. Brother, fast, run, house and snake are the words you should give him.

Write down the number he got correct here.

Part IV

In this section you are interested in words that end with the same sounds as the key words you give him. Ask him to listen very carefully and then say, "If I said sorry what word could you give me that ends with that same sound? O.K. Since I said sorry, you could have said fairy or sunny or carry. These words all end with the same sound."

Present the following words to your child without emphasizing the ending sound. If he does not seem to understand you may go back over the directions with him a maximum of two or more times. Allow about five seconds for his response to each word. Here are the words: Mom, sob, dot, drop, pen. Write number correct here.

Part V

On this last part of the Index you should sit down next to your child so that he can look at the book with you. Then say, "We are going to look at some letters together. I am going to point to each of them and say its name and then ask you to say its sound."

Allow about 5 seconds for each letter or letter combination and give him only one chance for each. (If you know that he is not ready for this exercise, you may leave *Part V* out altogether.)

In giving the letters or letter combinations to your child, say their names, not their sounds. You may use the following key in presenting the letters. Say, "Listen carefully and give me the sound of the letters as I name them to you. The *b* as it sounds in *bat*; the *c* as it sounds in *cat*; the *d* as it sounds in *dog*; the *f* as in *fish*; the *h* as in *house*; the *m* as in *mother*; *n* as in *nut*; *p* as in *pat*; *r* as in *rat*; *s* as in *snake*; *t* as in *tank*; *sh* as in *ship*; *th* as in *that*; *wh* as in *wheel*; and the *ch* as in *church*." (In using the key words, use them clearly without undue emphasis. Do not say their sounds. Tell your child you want him to give you the sound of each letter or letter combination as it sounds in each key word. Tell him it will be the first sound he will hear.)

Score each correct sound he says as one point and write the score below. Then add all of the scores from all parts of this Index and write the grand total on the first page of this Index. Score

INTERPRETATION AND USE OF THE SOUNDING STATUS INDEX

Research into what reading is all about seems to tell us that before a child can learn to read he must be able to hear differences among spoken speech sounds. The information you just obtained and received in the form of a score telling the number of responses your child got correct gives us an idea of his standing with regard to this indispensable pre-reading skill. Since each part of the Index requires a little more skill in hearing differences in sounds than the part preceding it, we can generally tell from his total score the degree of proficiency he has achieved. (An average score on this inventory is between 15 and 20.) This is, again, important information which we will need later to match your child to the most probable beneficial approach with which to begin reading instruction.

DESCRIPTION OF THE SOCIAL FLEXIBILITIES APPRAISAL

This is the last piece of information we will need prior to reading the Generic History-Observations and then deciding which beginning reading approach to use with your child. You do not need to have your child complete this final part of the Evaluation Section. All you need is a few quiet moments with a pencil and this book at a writing table or desk.

Since you alone are completing this section, the procedure varies from the one used for the other inventories. First of all, please do not preview this inventory or the way it is scored until you have completed it. In completing it, be as *objective and fair* as you can because it's meaningful later use depends on these critical factors.

Social Flexibilities Appraisal

Answer each question below by checking the appropriate blank. (x)

1. Does your child play with many other children regularly? Yes _____ No _____
2. Does he have more than one close playmate at any one time? Yes _____ No _____
3. Does your child attend any kind of school? Yes _____ No _____
4. Will your child try something new (like roller skating) on his own? Yes _____ No _____

46

5. Does your child usually dress on his own? Yes _____
No _____

6. Will he admit to making errors? Yes _____ No _____

7. Does he get excited when thinking of going on a trip?
Yes _____ No _____

8. Does he look at picture books some of the time by
himself? Yes _____ No _____

9. Does he behave fairly well around children he does not
particularly care for? Yes _____ No _____

10. Is your child fairly independent when others are not
around? Yes _____ No _____

11. Does he go to the bathroom on his own? Yes _____
No _____

12. Is your child a leader? Yes _____ No _____

13. Does he play with children of the opposite sex? Yes_
No _____

14. Is your child usually fairly healthy? Yes _____
No _____

15. Does he cry much? Yes _____ No _____

16. Does he have any adult hero other than someone in
the immediate family? Yes _____ No _____

17. Does he take turns? Yes _____ No _____

18. Does your child know how many objects he really
would have if he had eight of something? Yes _____
No _____

19. Does he ever question the reality of Bugs Bunny?
Yes _____ No _____

20. Does he know the difference between "evening" and
"morning"? Yes _____ No _____

21. Does he take part in competitive games? Yes _____
No _____

22. Is your child generally happy while at home? Yes _____
No _____

23. Does he often have temper tantrums? Yes _____
No _____

24. Does he speak favorably of neighborhood or other friends when they are not around?   Yes ____ No ____

SCORING, INTERPRETATION, AND USE OF THE SOCIAL FLEXIBILITIES APPRAISAL

While completing the appraisal you no doubt noted the questions were based on two general themes: (1) child interaction with his neighborhood or other friends and (2) his own individual maturity level.

Generally, in completing this appraisal, you have formulated a picture of your preschooler in a social situation. Due to numerous variabilities, however, no concrete picture or pass-fail evaluation can be imposed. Authorities however, do list certain characteristics of this age child in a new learning situation. Your youngster is coming to a new phase in his life. He is about to begin a structured learning problem for the first time and to be put into a situation in which he can no longer depend entirely upon you. Learning to read is an individual process. Therefore, it is extremely important to have some quantified idea with regard to your child's social readiness or flexibility potential when encountering a new structured learning situation for the first time.

We are now ready to score the Social Flexibilities Appraisal. Score the Appraisal on the basis of the number of *yes* responses you gave and assign a score by using the following table.

Social Flexibilities Scoring Table

Number of Yes responses	Appraisal Score
0 to 7	I
8 to 13	II
14 to 19	III
20 to 24	IV

Record your score to the Appraisal in the form of a Roman numeral here.

SUMMARY OF THE EVALUATION SECTION

You have obtained quite a bit of information concerning your child which you are going to use very shortly in selecting the most probable adequate beginning reading approach to use with him. You can relax a little bit now because you have just completed the most difficult and technical work you will be asked to do in this book.

Now, in order to keep the scores you obtained in a convenient place so that you can refer to them as you read the Generic History-Observations, please record them in the appropriate blanks on the following Score Profile.

SCORE PROFILE

Inventory	*Scores*
Listening Levels Measure	(Paragraph letter here)
Pre-Reading Stages Inventory-Stage 1	a (number with a here)
Stage 2	b (number with b here)
Stage 3	c (number with c here)
Stage 4	d (number with d here)
Stage 5	e (number with e here)
Sounding Status Index	(Total number of correct sounds here)
Social Flexibilities Appraisal	(Total number of yes responses)

49

Once you have recorded the scores on the Scores Profile, note the page number since you will need to refer to this page again after reading the *green* section, the Generic History-Observation portion. It is coming up next.

Chapter Three

Step II

The Generic History-Observation Section

INTRODUCTION

The basic purpose of this section is to help you find the description of a preschool child learning to read which is most representative of your child and his learning-teaching situation. The following composite descriptions were taken from real life situations. All of the children you encounter in this section learned to read or were much better prepared for beginning reading before entering the first grade.

Once you have determined which Generic History-Observation most closely corresponds to your own child and situation, you will be directed to one of the four approach emphasis to early beginning reading instruction in the Blue section of this book. You will also note that allowances have been made should the first approach

51

emphasis you select appear inappropriate in your situation. In other words, because the teaching of reading and its theoretical underpinnings comprise more or less a "soft science", options have been incorporated which permit you to use an alternative method with your child should you and he not make the progress you feel you should be making. However, I would interject a note of caution here in the form of the much quoted phrase: "Patience is the key to success".

I would point out here that it would be an almost impossible task without seeing and talking with you and your child — and even then we could not be absolutely certain — to suggest a teaching approach emphasis to beginning reading that would be a sure-fire one everytime. Perhaps it is the time at this point, to reiterate the basic premise of this book, that these approach emphases do work with very young children and that furthermore, specific approach emphases do seem to work better with specific types of children and learning situations.

Keeping these statements in mind then, let us proceed to the Generic History-Observations.

GENERIC HISTORY-OBSERVATION-ONE
Family Background

Danny Smith is a white, male, Roman catholic aged five years, seven months. He is the fifth of seven children. Of his siblings, two of his brothers and two of his sisters are older.

Danny's father is a plumbing contractor and his mother is a nurse. The family lives in a five bedroom single family dwelling in a good residential section of a village with a population of some one hundred-twenty-one thousand.

The combined family income is slightly in excess of fifty thousand dollars per annum.

Danny's birth was normal and his health, including his vision and hearing, are within normal limits. Danny has always been a "good" boy in that he is obedient, unselfish, kind to his many neighborhood friends and is generally self-reliant and something of a leader. He gets along with his brothers and sisters and appears to be relatively happy with his life.

Danny has accompanied his family on a number of vacations and other trips and is quite familiar with the cultural and recreational facilities available in his community and its environs. He has had access to a number of childrens' books which he had learned to handle properly and knows something of reading since he has had ample opportunity to see his older siblings so engaged and has even had them, on various occasions, reading to him.

SCORES PROFILE

Inventory	Scores
Listening Levels Measures	T
Pre-Reading Stages Inventory—Stage 1	3a
Stage 2	2b
Stage 3	3c
Stage 4	3d
Stage 5	2e
Sounding Status Index	30
Sound Flexibilities Appraisal	IV

READING PROCEDURES

Danny's history indicates that he has been (1) exposed to a variety of reading materials; (2) read to by various members of the family; (3) probably given all of the creature comforts; (4) exposed to a wide variety of travel and recreational experiences; (5) generally physically well; (6) granted a degree of independence; and (7) usually fairly happy in his home situation.

His Scores Profile appear to reflect his relatively good home background. His score of T on the Listening Levels indicates that he is quite capable of profiting from reading instruction in general while 3's in three of the five stages and 2's in stages 2 and 5 indicate that he is generally ready for reading instruction. The score of /30 on the Sounding Status Index demonstrates a superior command of sounds while the score of IV on the Sound Flexibilities Appraisal indicates a child quite mature enough to cope with the reading process.

As a consequence, Danny's prognosis with respect to his ability to profit from reading instruction is rated superior. His mother would begin reading instruction by turning to the blue section and the approach emphasis labeled Memory Unit Form. If this approach does not appear to begin to achieve the desired goal within a month or so, his mother would then turn to the Sound Syntax Teaching Approach Emphasis.

GENERIC HISTORY OBSERVATION-TWO

John Martin became five years of age several months ago. He remembered his mother saying something about it and telling him that she was a very lucky mother and that a very nice present would be forthcoming just as soon as she got the dependents' check from John's father. John hoped that this time his father, whom he remembered seeing only a few times, would get the check to his mother for this occasion.

John felt that times always seemed better when the check did come because his mother did not seem so busy doing "domestic work" for white people and she spent more time with him and his two older brothers.

When John's mother was away working, he stayed at home with his grandmother in their three-room walk-up apartment. John really loved some of the things his grandmother did with him during the day when she and he were alone. One of his favorite things was when she told him stories of far away places and of the large stores she had been in downtown. John had never been too many places except in his imagination. The farthest he had ever been from his front door was last summer when he went downtown with his grandmother to visit Uncle Jack.

The only reading materials John saw around the house were some school books his older brothers brought home. He did not particularly care for them because his brothers said they were "dumb" and "for sissies."

SCORES PROFILE

Inventory	Scores
Listening Levels Measure	P
Pre-Reading Stages Inventory—Stage 1	1a
Stage 2	1b
Stage 3	1c
Stage 4	1d
Stage 5	1e
Sounding Status Index	9
Social Flexibilities Appraisal	II

READING PROCEDURES

John's observation shows that he has not been exposed to reading materials in any kind of positive fashion. This history also indicates that he has had very little opportunity to obtain experiences other than those circumscribed by the walls of his apartment. Furthermore, with the exception of listening to his grandmother's stories, John had not derived a great deal of enjoyment from relatively structured speech situations. John's scores profile tends to reinforce the information acquired from the family background. The score of P on the Listening Levels Measure indicates that his reading potential is good. However, the row of ones he obtained on the Pre-Reading Stages Inventory, his low score on the Sounding Status Index, and his low score on the Social Flexibilities Appraisal indicate that he will probably not profit from beginning reading instruction at this time.

Consequently, John's tutor referred to the Voice Impress-Look Along Approach Emphasis in the Blue section. John needs a variety of pre-reading experiences and activities which can best be given through this approach emphasis.

GENERIC HISTORY OBSERVATION-THREE
Family Background

Samuel Simmons is a white, male, Protestant aged four years and seven months. He is an only child in good general health. He lives in an apartment in a fairly high rent district where he is well cared for and happy.

Sam's father is a thirty-seven year old junior executive with a promising future in a large industrial firm and his mother is a college educated housewife. Sam's father at present, earns between fifteen and twenty thousand dollars a year, depending upon the amount of incentive bonuses given by the company.

Both parents are anxious for their only son to excel in all things and they push for this. At the same time they are both quite protective and sometimes, so their friends say, too easy-going with Sam.

Sam has traveled widely with his parents on vacations and has a great supply of reading materials. He usually "gets his way" with his parents and playmates and has not been overly encouraged to "do for himself." Sam is very alert and often takes part in adult conversations. He spends a great deal of time with his mother and is his father's "buddy."

He is quite interested in leafing through picture books and loves to hear his mother read to him. Although, during these occasions his attention does wander so that about five minutes is all that he will closely attend at any given time.

SCORES PROFILE

Inventory	*Scores*
Listening Levels Measure	R
Pre-Reading Stages Inventory—Stage 1	2a
Stage 2	3b
Stage 3	3c
Stage 4	3c
Stage 5	2e
Sounding Status Index	25
Social Flexibilities Appraisal	I

READING PROCEDURES

The Scores Profile indicates that Sam's reading potential is quite good. The Pre-reading stages inventory and the Sounding Status Index tell us that he can cope with beginning reading instruction and that he is verbally well prepared. However, the Social Flexibilties Appraisal score of I informs us that he is not socially ready for such instruction.

Information from the family background section appears to substantiate the knowledge we have gained from the Social Flexibilties Appraisal. Sam seems to be a child who is generally socially immature. This immaturity manifests itself in his relatively poor peer association, his excessive reliance on his parents, and his short attention span.

As a result of this information, Sam's mother turned to the Voice Impress-Look Along Approach Emphasis in the Blue section. When he became more socially mature and could attend a structured learning situation for a longer period of time and could also complete certain experience activities "on his own," his mother turned to the Memory Unit Form Teaching Approach Emphasis.

GENERIC HISTORY-OBSERVATION-FOUR
Family Background

Jill Matthews is a five and one half year old white, Protestant, female of excellent health. She lives in an upper middle class neighborhood in a single unit family dwelling. Her father is a successful lawyer and her mother is a college educated housewife. Jill is the oldest of three children.

Both of Jill's parents are in their late thirties, aggressive, and well liked in their suburb of New York City. Jill has always been extremely well provided for, is loved dearly by her family, and gets along well with her few playmates whom she always obeys and follows without question. She has traveled considerably, is read to often, and is always included in family conversation.

Jill likes to play alone and does not seem to learn so quickly as her younger sisters. She was slow in developing her speech, having uttered her first complete sentence when she was four years of age. She does not dress herself, cannot seem to learn to count to ten meaningfully and seems generally slow and meticulous in life's activities.

She is attractive, very affectionate, kind, generally unspontaneous in her behavior, and extremely appreciative of all the attention that is paid her. When she learns a task for the first time, she becomes quite excited and tends to repeat it any number of times. Her playmates treat her well, but tend to ignore her at these times when they are engaged in games demanding fine physical coordination and relatively complex verbal behavior.

SCORES PROFILE

Inventory	Scores
Listening Levels Measure	N
Pre-Reading Stages Inventory—Stage 1	2a
Stage 2	2b
Stage 3	1c
Stage 4	1d
Stage 5	1e
Sounding Status Index	14
Social Flexibilities Appraisal	III

READING PROCEDURES

Jill's family background history indicates that while she has been exposed to many reading activites and a broad range of experience opportunities, she has not profited from these to the degree that many other children have and would. Her family background is such that she has been encouraged to respond favorably to reading situations and materials. In addition, Jill is attentive and tends to pursue a task until she masters it, and once having mastered it very seldom forgets it. However, her skill and task mastery seem to be characterized by a slowness and a necessity for numerous repetitions.

Her Scores Profile bears out the information obtained from her family background history. Her Listening Levels Measure score indicates that, for the present time at least, her reading potential or capacity is quite limited.

The scores obtained from Jill's Pre-Reading Stages Inventory show that she is aware of and can make visual discriminations among shapes and pictures fairly well and that her vocabulary and ability to follow directions is also about average. However, the Pre-Reading Stages Inventory also indicates that she has limited skills in matching and in isolating and identifying letters and words. Her score on the Sounding Status Index demonstrates that while she does have some skill in making and noting similarities and differences in spoken sounds this too, is not highly developed. And finally, her Social Flexibilities Appraisal score indicates that she is socially mature enough to benefit from beginning reading instruction.

Jill's mother was asked to use the Visual-Motor-Touch-Approach Emphasis in the Blue section. She was referred to this approach because Jill needs the reading task to be made as specific and concrete as possible. Her mother was also told that if moderate success was not forthcoming from this approach within two or three months, to try the Voice Impress-Look Along Emphasis.

GENERIC HISTORY-OBSERVATION-FIVE
Family Background

My name is Bill Carter and I live in the big brick house on Vista Lane. I am almost six years old. I have a brother and a sister older than me and another sister younger. I have a dog, a cat, and a mother and father who "bug" me a lot. In fact, when my father isn't uptown doing office work, he is yelling at me just like my mother who is always telling me to be good.

60

I don't think anyone likes me very well. My family is always fighting me and so do my friends, if you can call them friends. People just won't stop "bugging" me. They really don't like me. I heard my mother telling my father that there must be something wrong with me because I am cruel to the dog and don't want to play nice with my brother and sisters or the neighborhood guys.

I just like to be by myself because others always start a fight with me. I don't like people paying attention to others when I am around, but they always do. But I make them sorry for that. I can read my picture books pretty well, but I would rather tear them up because they are no good. In fact, there aren't many good things around.

SCORES PROFILE

Inventory	Scores
Listening Levels Measure	u-u
Pre-Reading Stages Inventory—Stage 1	2a
Stage 2	3b
Stage 3	3c
Stage 4	2d
Stage 5	3e
Sounding Status Index	27
Social Flexibilities Appraisal	I

READING PROCEDURES

The Scores Profile indicates that Bill has truly superior reading potential and that he could benefit from beginning reading instruction. The problem here, of course, is whether Bill wants to learn to read. His inconsistent scores on the Pre-Reading Stages Inventory and his inability to work independently as well as his general perspective on life would seem to preclude any kind of beginning reading instruction at this time.

Bill is severely emotionally disturbed. Although this maladjustment is not reflected by his Scores Profile to any extent, it certainly is in his family history.

Consequently, further use of this book with Bill was not recommended at this time. Instead, Bill's parents took him to the family physician who in turn informed them of a specialist who could help Bill and his parents work through the situation.

GENERIC-HISTORY OBSERVATION - SIX
Family Background

Will and his four brothers and sisters have lived in a variety of one bedroom apartments since they had moved into the inner city from their rural farm. Despite the difficulties that their lives have weathered, the entire family has remained together.

The boy is the third child in a family of four children. There are two older sisters and a younger brother. The oldest child, Rita, has striven hard to keep ahead of her siblings. Not only has she been asked, frequently, to assume caring for all of the children, but thrives on being in control over her siblings. Will is often the target of her wrath. Under Rita's unrelenting shadow, the boy has not been allowed the advantages of praise and independent accomplishment. On the other hand, Will is compliant and seems content in being so. He depends almost completely on others to set the tone of his life.

Recently, there have been occasions when Will has refused to leave his mother's or his sister's side. Another time he refused to attend a birthday party for a young friend, and still another was when an attempt was made to enroll him in a neighborhood Bible School. Will's resistance was overwhelming and won out in the end.

Will has not spent much time with crayons, pencils, paper, etc. What few opportunities there were have been interrupted by Rita. She usually "finished" his pictures or would draw what was requested by him.

Next year he will enter kindergarten with 28 other children.

SCORES PROFILE

Inventory	Scores
Listening Levels Measure	0
Pre-Reading Stages Inventory—Stage 1	2a
Stage 2	1b
Stage 3	1c
Stage 4	1d
Stage 5	1e
Sounding Status Index	18
Social Flexibilities Appraisal	I

READING PROCEDURES

Will's family history indicates that while he has experienced a variety of household moves, he has not really had too much opportunity to benefit from them. The history further tells us that he appears to be overshadowed by an older sister who seems to steal his pre-reading successes from him.

Will's score on the Pre-Reading Status Inventory and the Social Flexibilities Approach reflect his family experiences in that they indicate that he is generally not ready to achieve success on his own insofar as beginning reading instruction is concerned. However, his Listening Levels Measure and his Sounding Status Index scores tell us that his reading potential is good and that he has an average grasp of sounds.

Will's primary problem in beginning reading instruction appears to be his general social immaturity and his lack of skill in telling differences among written symbols (Pre-Reading Stages Inventory). Consequently, Will's mother turned to the Visual-Motor-Touch Approach Emphasis in the Blue section and continued with this approach through the First Phase Reader. At that time, Will demonstrated he could make visual discrimination and that he could work independently. She then began utilizing the Second Phase Reader.

GENERIC HISTORY-OBSERVATION-SEVEN
Family Background

Linda Spike is nearly six years of age. She is white, the child of Jewish parents who are living together. She has a sister two years older than herself and brother three years younger. Her father is a dentist, and her mother is a trained elementary school teacher who had taught only one year before getting married. The family resides in an exclusive subdivision mostly inhabited by professional people. The small community tends to be insular because it's size precludes the existence of cultural events of high caliber. Linda's health is excellent and she eagerly anticipated learning to read like her older sister whom she admires and imitates.

Linda has had many travel and other experiences and has been read to frequently. She has an ample supply of picture books which she "reads" avidly. Linda can relate the picture and oral stories she encounters in sequential order and seems to comprehend them. However, although her hearing is excellent, what she relates is sometimes a little difficult to understand since she speaks with a lisp and occasionally, confuses initial beginning and ending sounds.

SCORES PROFILE

Inventory	Scores
Listening Levels Measure	P
Pre-Reading Stages Inventory—Stage 1	3a
Stage 2	3b
Stage 3	2c
Stage 4	3d
Stage 5	3c
Sounding Status Index	8
Social Flexibilities Appraisal	IV

READING PROCEDURES

Linda's family background indicates that she has been exposed to a wide variety of pre-reading experiences and that she has related positively to them. There is also an indication that she can retell what she hears in a logical order but that she evidences an articulatory problem which manifests itself primarily in her inability to pronounce the R sound. She also confuses beginning and ending sounds in her speech at times even though a physical examination indicated that her hearing acuity (sharpness) was normal.

Linda's Scores Profile indicates that she is ready to profit from beginning reading instructions with the exception of the Sounding Status Index score which is well below the average of 15. Since her other scores indicate a readiness to begin and because her problems in sounding are probably due to a lack of conscious practice in making the sounds and to speech immaturity, Linda's mother was referred to the Sound Syntax Teaching Approach Emphasis in the Blue section. She was asked to work with Linda using this approach emphasis until Linda began to make beginning and ending sounds without confusing them through the First Phase Reader. (Linda's mother was asked not to be concerned about her lisp.)

REVIEW AND CONTINUATION OF GENERIC HISTORY OBSERVATIONS

Before continuing with the remaining abbreviated Generic History Observations, let's pause momentarily and review a few basic points common to all of the preceding histories.

First, the children described on the preceding and following pages could be from one or several families. The descriptions have been made inclusive enough so as to apply to the many children that the writer has come in contact with. Each history presents unique circumstances of, readiness levels for, and resultant learning styles of the child characterized.

Secondly, the history observations stress the significance of travel experiences, book handling experiences, listening to stories, peer relationships, family togetherness, parental-child relationships, attention span and level of independence. All of these factors are taken into consideration along with the child's Scores Profile.

Now that you have a general idea of the points considered in the family background section and their relationship to the Scores Profile, please read the remaining Generic History Observations. When you begin, you will note that they are more abbreviated than the preceding seven. This was done at this point because you are more aware of what to note in the histories and in order to save you time.

GENERIC HISTORY OBSERVATION-EIGHT

Name   Fred Goldfarb

Age   5.0

Sex	Male
Race	White
Religion	Jewish
Siblings	1 younger brother ; 1 older sister
Father's Occupation	M.D.
Mother's Occupation	Former high school English teacher
Home Situation	Very happy except for intrusion of babysitter daily
Residential Setting	High-average suburbs
Others in the Home	None
Health	Excellent
Comments	In their anxiety to make their child an above- average student, Fred's parents have tried to teach him to read and write at home. His practice sessions on his blackboard have revealed, however, that he makes certain letters backwards and reverses the r and e in his name.
Scores Profile	Listening Levels Measure O
	Pre-Reading Stages Inventory 2a, 2b, 2c, 2d, 1e
	Sounding Status Index 21
	Social Flexibilities Appraisal III

67

Fred's mother faces the task of correcting an already established habit. Her one consolation is that Fred is young and has several years to make amends, but she is at a disadvantage in that first impressions are lasting ones, and Fred's progress will have to be checked very closely during his first few years of reading.

The procedure for correction involves emphasizing left to right sequential order and other activities utilizing the Visual Motor Touch Teaching Approach Emphasis. Fred's mother will continue with this approach with Fred until he no longer makes reversals. At that time she will move to the balanced approach in the Second Phase Reader.

GENERIC HISTORY OBSERVATION-NINE

Name	Carol Blythe
Age	5.8
Sex	Female
Race	Black
Religion	Baptist
Siblings	1 younger child
Father's Occupation	High school physics teacher
Mother's Occupation	Elementary teacher
Home Situation	Very happy
Residential Setting	Apartment complex in an average suburban neighborhood
Others in the Home	None

Health	Excellent
Comments	Carol has shown signs of being very alert. She takes an active part in neighborhood play and is considered a leader by her peers. Her parents have tried to prepare her for reading by familiarizing her with books and pictures. However, she seems to have a great deal of difficulty in learning and remembering letter sounds.
Scores Profile	Listening Levels Measure q Pre-Reading Stages Inventory 3a, 3b, 2c, 2d, 3e Sounding Status Index 9 Social Flexibilities Appraisal IV

Carol will learn to read with the Sound-Syntax Approach Emphasis. This emphasis was selected for her in view of her difficulty with letter sounds, her reading potential, her general readiness, and her ability to work independentiy. In brief, the primary reason for using Sound Syntax with this particular child is that she has already become anxious about reading. Her parents have instilled in her the excitement of reading stories and since she does not have the necessary sounding skills this approach will afford her the fastest possible basic preparation. When Carol has mastered the basic sounds, her mother will then proceed to the balanced approach emphasis in the Second Phase Reader.

GENERIC HISTORY OBSERVATION-TEN

Name	Tom Roberts
Age	4.10

Sex	Male
Race	Black
Religion	Methodist
Siblings	None
Father's Occupation	Department store superintendent
Mother's Occupation	Housewife
Home Situation	Good
Residential Setting	Average
Others in the Home	One uncle
Health	Good
Comments	Tom's parents have expressed concern as to their son's probable reading success when he goes to school. He is an effervescent child - to the point of being annoying at times. His attention span is critically short and he demands almost constant activity. Tom's parents are apprehensive because they fear that he cannot adapt to the formalities and restraints of the impending kindergarten situation.
Scores Profile	Listening Levels Measure N
	Pre-Reading Stages Inventory 2a, 1b, 1c, 1d, 1e

The approach appropriate for Tom is the Voice Impress-Look Along Emphasis. It involves listening and oral expression in addition to being a "fun" type of reading activity. The added voice participation will aid Tom in releasing some of his excess energy. When Tom has "settled down" somewhat and is paying attention, his mother will then turn to the Sound-Syntax Approach and begin using this with him.

COMPLETING YOUR CHILD'S GENERIC HISTORY FORM

Now that you have read the Generic History Observations you probably have a good idea as to which approach emphasis to select for your child. Do not become dismayed, however, if every behavioral aspect of your child is not represented in any one Generic History-Observation. Remember, it was stated earlier that it would be virtually impossible to completely portray your child since every human being is unique. In every sense, the meaning of the phrase, "after his creation the mold was thrown away" is true in this case. Your child is one of a kind.

Nonetheless, you can study the Generic History Observations and then select the one that most closely resembles your own unique child and his learning situation. If you will complete the form provided on the following pages, you will probably be able to resolve any uncertainty you may have with regard to which approach emphasis to use. When completing this form be certain to reread the appropriate sections of the history observations when you are not sure of a specific response.

THE INDIVIDUAL GENERIC HISTORY-OBSERVATION *(YOUR CHILD)*

Name ————————————— Date —————————————

Mo. ——— Day ——— Year —

Age _____ years _____ months   Date of Birth _____
                                          Mo.   Day   Yr.

Section One

Complete the statements below by selecting the most appropriate word from the parenthesis following each item.

    1. My child's health is generally _____
       (good, fair, poor)

    2. His vision seems to be _____
       (good, fair, poor)

    3. His hearing seems to be _____
       (good, fair, poor)

Please note that if you are not certain about your child's general health including his hearing or vision, please have him examined by a physician.

    4. My child's speech is generally _____
       (good, fair, poor)

    5. I understand what he says _____
       (most of the time, some of the time, hardly ever)

    6. The number of words in his vocabulary is _____
       (high, medium, low)

    7. The use of complete sentences in his speech is _____
       (high, medium, low)

Section Two

Complete the following section by checking (x) the appropriate yes or no blank at the end of each question.

1. Does you child want to learn to read? Yes _____
   No _____

2. Does your child have access to a number of picture and reading materials? Yes _____ No _____

3. Does your child ask you to read to him often? Yes ___
   No _____

4. Have you read to him and told him meaningful stories?
   Yes _____ No _____

5. Has your child visited places of interest to him, such as zoos, museums, parks, etc.? Yes _____ No _____

6. Have you taken your child to a public library? Yes ___
   No _____

7. Does he have other brothers and sisters who enjoy reading and have told him so? Yes _____ No _____

8. Does you child like to "read" on his own? Yes _____
   No _____

9. Has your child ever visited a school? Yes _____ No ___

10. Does he want to go to school when he is old enough?
    Yes _____ No _____

Section one and two along with the score from the Social Flexibilities Appraisal correspond to the family background sections of the Generic History Observations. Thus, after completing these two sections, you need to review your Social Flexibilities Appraisal by looking again at each of the questions and your answers. Generally speaking, the more positive your answers were on the two sections and the higher the score on the Social Flexibilities Appraisal, the more prepared your child is in terms of social, physical, and attitudinal maturity to undertake beginning reading instruction.

However, these sections and the scores do not necessarily give you any information concerning your child's academic or word manipulation in learning to read. The Scores Profile, in Section Three of this form will give you an indication of this.

Section Three

You have already recorded all of the inventory scores on the Scores Profile. Please refer to that page again at this time and record those requested once more below.

Listening Levels Index

Pre-Reading Inventory: Visual Discrimination, Stage

Vocabulary and Following Instructions, Stage 2

Letter Symbols Cross Out, Stage 3

Letter Symbols Matching, Stage 4

Identification of Symbols and Units, Stage 5

Sounding Status Index

(You will note that the Social Flexibilities Appraisal was not asked for here again since you have already used it in Section Two).

Please recall it was stated that the Listening Levels Index score was administered to give you an idea as to your child's comprehension of speech, academic or "book learning" readiness, and his general reading potential or what difficulty level of reading material he could understand if he could read. If your child is three to four years of age, he did well if he made an N or more. If he is four to five, he did all right if he got an 0 or above and if he is five to six, he is ready if he made a P or more.

In looking at the Pre-Reading Stages Inventory, of course the higher the score for each stage, the more likely your child will profit from beginning reading instruction. This inventory gives you an idea of your child's skill in seeing differences among written picture forms, letters and words. Obviously he must be able to see to some extent that there are differences among various written forms before he can learn to read.

In general, if your child is three to four years of age, he should have made at least two scores of two or one score of 3. If he is four to five he should have gotten at least three scores of 2 or two scores of 3. If he is 5 to 6 he should make three scores of 2 or better and at least one score of 3.

The Sounding Status Index

The Sounding Status Index score gives an idea as to how well your child does in hearing differences among spoken sounds. This ability or skill, as in seeing differences, is a basic necessity if he is to learn to read. If your child, regardless of his age, made a score of at least 18 on this inventory, he has the ability to discriminate among speech sounds and may be ready to profit from beginning reading instruction provided his other scores are adequate.

Section Four

This section attempts to relate all of the numbers from the Scores Profile to the information obtained from sections two and three, (family background information) in an effort to tie the separate pieces together so that you can use it to definitely select a Teaching Approach Emphasis.

As a note of caution, the following statements should not be considered prescriptive. They are general in nature only. In the final analysis you, as the prospective teacher, must decide on the basis of the more detailed information you have obtained to date through the use of this book what specific teaching approach emphasis you are going to use. If your child's Social Flexibilities Appraisal is I and your responses to sections one and two of this form are forty percent or more negative, regardless of his age, try the Voice Impress-Look Along Teaching Approach Emphasis. Likewise, you will want to try this approach emphasis if his scores on the Pre-Reading Stages Inventory and the Sounding Status Index are below the minimum for his age as reported in section three.

Other general statements concerning the combining of the Scores Profiles and the Generic History Observation in order to select the appropriate approach emphasis have been summarized and are presented in tabular form in the General Statement Table below.

In reading the table, the pluses (+) refer to an adequate score for a child depending on his age while the minuses (-) refer to scores not quite up to par. The labels across the top of the table refer to the child's age, his scores from his Scores Profile, and your answers to sections 1 and 2 of this form, your personal History-Observation, and the suggested teaching approach emphasis. For example, in looking at the top first row across we see that a child between the ages of 3 and 6 who made a below average score for his age on listening and average or above average scores on pre-reading, sounding, social flexibility, and 60 per cent or more yes responses on sections one and two of this form should begin reading instruction using the Visual-Motor-Touch Teaching Approach Emphasis.

Please note that these are general statements only. They are provided here to give you an idea of how you combine information from the Generic History Observations and on your Scores Profile and on your individual History Observation in order to select an approach emphasis. They are for purposes of illustration only.

You have now compiled all of the detailed information you have acquired concerning your child on your individual Generic History

General Statement Table

Age	Listening	Pre-Reading	Sounds	Flexibilities	Sections 1 & 2	Approach
3-6	-	+	+	+	+	Visual-Motor Touch
3-6	+	-	-	-	-	Voice-Impress Look Along
5-6	+	+	-	+	+	Sound Syntax
3-6	+	+	+	+	+	Memory-Unit Form
3-6	+	-	+	+	+	Visual-Motor Touch
3-6	+	-	-	+	+	Voice-Impress Look Along
3-6	+	+	+	+	-	Memory-Unit Form
5-6	-	+	-	+	+	Sound-Syntax
5-6	-	-	+ or -	+	+	Visual-Motor Touch

Form to decide on which teaching approach emphasis to use. Review the Generic History Observations most like your child, reread the information you have in sections one, two, three and four of the Individualized Generic History Observation Form and make your decision. *Decide on the teaching approach emphasis now* and then take a break.

Section Five

Now that you have selected a teaching approach emphasis turn to the Blue section and read the introduction to all of the teaching approach emphases and then turn to the one you have chosen and read it carefully. When you have finished, please summarize the approach emphasis you have selected in the space provided below in five sentences or less. If you are not sure you are ready to do this, please go back and reread the description of your selected emphasis again.

Summary of   Teaching
Approach Emphasis

After you have finished your summary, congratulate yourself. In only a few moments more, you will be ready to begin teaching your child to read. You have just a couple of more pages to read. Turn to the trial teaching example where you will find some things you will probably want to say to your child to help him get ready to read.

Notes on your child's personal history.

Notes

Notes

Notes

Chapter Four

Step III

The Teaching Approach Emphases Section

INTRODUCTION

Before studying the approach emphasis you have been referred to, it is quite important that you carefully read the following introductory paragraphs. In learning to read there are four categories of child-attained experiences which are absolutely essential, regardless of approach-emphasis, if the child is to achieve reading success. These experience categories which the child must have profited from and so developed some proficiencies in, include skills in: (1) attentive listening; (2) adequate oral language usage; (3) left to right sequence; and (4) some letter name symbol and sound correspondence acquaintance. A discussion of each of these categories comprises the main part of this introduction.

We will consider the skill of listening attentively first of all. It has been stated that a child listens in about the same fashion as others listen to him. If we accept this premise, it follows that we will listen to our children with courtesy and close attention. If you have adopted this procedure as a policy in your home, you are not likely to encounter any great difficulty on this point.

If you feel that your child may be lacking in this important skill to the degree that you cannot keep his sustained attention for more than three or four minutes, it is suggested that you work with him in the Gray section of this book before going on to one of the approach emphases. The child should be able to give you his undivided attention and show you that he has by responding meaningfully for at least seven or eight minutes at a time. By responding meaningfully, I mean that he demonstrates to you, by answering in an understanding fashion, any questions you ask him concerning the topic you and he were considering during the time he was supposed to be listening attentively.

Secondly, your child must possess a certain level of competency in oral language usage. Here, you need not be overly concerned with articulatory (word pronouncing) mode or an extensive speaking vocabulary. The main point is that you can understand what he says and he understands what you say and that he can speak in complete sentences when he wants to and that he knows a number of different everyday words. Once again, you will want to use the Gray section if there is a great lack in this language usage area. Generally speaking, if your child understands your language (for example, he understands spoken directions by following through on them) and others not in the family understand what he is saying most of the time, and he can string words together to make at least short sentences, he is all right on this score and you can go ahead with the designated approach emphasis.

The third skill area your child must know something about is that of left to right sequence. In other words, he must know that when people read, they read from left to right and from one line of print or picture to the next line of print or pictures located directly beneath the preceding line. Obviously, you can tell this about your child by observing when he is looking at a picture book, magazine, and so forth.

If he seems to be experiencing difficulty in this area, you will need to work with him some in the Gray section before going on to the appropriate approach emphasis. This skill usually does not require much time to develop and so it should not hold you up very long. The important thing here is to make sure that your child knows this is the way one always goes about reading pictures, stories, and books. So keep your eye on him with regard to this and remind him when necessary.

The fourth skill area your child must have some experience in concerns phoneme to grapheme and grapheme to phoneme correspondence. All this means is that he must be able to see, when pointed out to him that the letter B, for example, is different from the letter D and that each one has a different name and a different sound. (But, while knowledge of the letter names is helpful, it is not essential and he does not need to know letter sounds at this time.) You already know your child's skill in this area from the scores he made on the Pre-Reading Stages Inventory and the Sounding Stages Index.

If your child did not do very well on these inventories, you will be using the Voice Impress-Look Along Teaching Approach Emphasis. I am simply reiterating at this point the importance of experience and skill development in this area.

These then, are the four experience areas your child must have some skill in if he is to learn to read successfully at this time. If he has some proficiency in these areas, he will learn to read just as quickly as you can teach him from this book.

You are about to read and study the approach emphasis you have selected to use with your child. Before doing so, there are a few final points you should keep in mind.

The approach emphases presented on the following pages are just what their name implies. They represent ways and places to begin the teaching of reading. Each approach emphasis stresses a specific way to begin teaching reading and is intended for a particular type of child.

Once you have studied the approach emphasis you have selected for your child, you will probably continue using it throughout the First Phase Reader. However, after successfully completing the First Phase Reader, your child will have the skills necessary to read with you the Second Phase Reader using a balanced and general approach which does not emphasize any particular reading element more than another. Thus, the approach emphasis you will use initially with your child will give way to a balanced and comprehensive general approach after your child has learned to read his first words and stories.

TEACHING APPROACH EMPHASIS I

Memory Unit Form

The rationale for this emphasis was drawn largely from the works of Gray, Gates, Smith and Dawson. In utilizing this approach emphasis with your child you first need to know how he will learn to differentiate among words and remember them. In general, he will learn to use visual characteristics of the total configuration or total shape of each word. Your primary task, then, is to help him develop sophisticated ways of looking at words. You can help him do this by emphasizing and discussing certain visual characteristics of words by pointing out how long they are, how tall, and how many letters extend above and below the line of point.

At the time you begin to use this approach emphasis with your child, he will be fairly proficient in the spoken language, but not with speech in written form. However, he has had (as evidenced by the Scores Profile, otherwise you should not be using this approach) considerable experience in "reading" pictures. Therefore, in teaching your child new words, if you first pronounce the word and help the child pronounce it by means of pictures (this has been automatically provided for you in the First Phase Reader), you will smooth the transition from speech to print.

Colorful pictures stimulate the child and aid him in learning to associate written symbols with their pictorial forms. By looking at the word and picture forms and thinking of your pronunciation of a given word, he learns to relate its spoken sound with its meaning and written shape as a total unit.

In using this approach with the First Phase Reader, be certain not to overstress review of a particular page since you will not typically expect him to be absolutely sure of a word after he sees it only one or two times. The First Phase Reader has incorporated this idea in that each word is repeated a number of times in a number of different contexts or story situations. However, to reinforce his learning of words, it would be a good idea if you had a number of beginning books which include these same words to give him practice in as many different contexts as possible.

In using this approach emphasis the idea is not merely to present the child with a number of stories or lists of words to memorize. You must teach him to react actively to the word form. By doing this you will eliminate future reading failure caused by his looking at a word in a haphazard fashion so that it makes no impression at all on him. This active reaction to word form will eventually promote rapid word recognition. When starting his study of word shape, he will need guidance in finding the most significant characteristics of the printed word, those characteristics which will be the most helpful in learning words. Initially, your child will see only large and obvious differences between words. For this reason he will depend upon word length, height, line overlap, and general word shape in the beginning. Later, these basic skills will comprise the foundation for more sophisticated skills. Therefore, the First Phase Reader has included many independent study exercises intended to develop these perceptual skills. (These are exercises which the child is asked to do on his own). The word length characteristic is important because your child will probably experience less difficulty in identifying and recalling words such as "armadillo" and "November" than words similar in shape such as "were", "where", "them", and "that". With continued practice in this approach emphasis, your child will recognize many more longer and more complex words than children taught other ways. The height characteristics of words are also quite helpful in learning to read. Here you need to point out height differences in words such as "for," "got," "big," and "cat" for example. The third characteristic, line overlap, also acts as a word learning sign. In using this characteristic you should point out the line overlap characteristics of words such as "pan," "dig," "spring," and "bag" for example.

In using these signs of unit form, it is probably better for your child to decide which characteristic of the word or unit form make the word identifiable for him. In teaching your child, let him tell you what he sees in the general shape of a word that helps him learn it, after you have explained directly to him the ideas of length, height and line overlap.

When new words are introduced to the child, they should be written on stationery or on cards so that he can see what it looks like through another medium. Here, you must be extremely careful to see that your printing is both consistent from day-to-day and legible. In presenting any given word, you can ask your child to match the new word with the correct word from a list you have written out. When teaching a story, you could also request him to find a new word on the page containing it after you have introduced it. In giving these kinds of exercises, you should provide accompanying discussions to add meaning to the job of learning words and later, phrases.

While the First Phase Reader avoids introducing too many new words in one sentence, you should present each new word in as many different forms as possible. For instance, in introducing a new word, you could present it to him in both its capital and small case forms. You will also need to help him to compare new words with old similar words to avoid possible confusion. To do this, point out (or have him point out) the similarities as well as the differences among the words. This practice will also permit you to review words introduced in the past.

You must use this approach emphasis systematically. Your child cannot be left to make hit or miss guesses at words, but must be taught carefully to develop his word identification skills. He must learn both *how* to look at words and how to note which characteristics will help him to identify them.

Care has been taken to assure that the First Phase Reader is appropriate to the child's level of achievement. You need to do the same by selecting his other reading materials so that he will not be exposed to more than one new word in every twenty.

Now that you have completed reading the description of the Memory Unit Form Teaching Approach Emphasis you may be wondering how you are to put it into practice. The next part of this approach emphasis section is intended to clarify the use of the approach by presenting a series of exercises which you will later be using with your child in conjunction with the First Phase Reader. However for the present, you are asked to read the exercises carefully and to refer to the first part of this approach description when you have a question.

MEMORY UNIT FORM EXERCISE MODELS

Remember, these are to be used as given activity models (after you have carefully studied them) *when, and as you are requested to do so in the teaching portion of the First Phase Reader.* Your child should not spend more than fifteen minutes on any one exercise.

-1-

Shape Identification
Directions: Present your child with a series of geometric shapes such as squares, triangles, rectangles, etc. Let him discover their differences and similarities. Teach him the names of the shapes and then ask him to draw or copy them.

-2-

Form Identification I
Directions: Trace a number of animals and ask your child to

identify them by their shapes. Start with animals of distinctive shape (mouse, dog) and work up to finer distinctions. For example the distinction between a bear and a wolf.

-3-

Form Identification II
    Directions: Show your child several pictures, each having a central figure with a distinctive shape. Prepare outline drawings of the central figures. After he has identified the pictures, present the outline only for him to identify.

-4-

Word-Pix Relationships

Write Your First Name Down There.   Draw Yourself Here.

(Ask mother to help you)

                                                    (Draw your word pictures here)

ants

crack

house

mouse

Directions: Tell him these are words which tell what the pictures are. Draw pictures of the words. Discuss the characteristics of each word. Let him color the pictures if he wants to. Review the words and pix with him until he tires.

-5-

Unit Configurations
Directions: Ask him to carefully draw the shape of each word on a piece of paper. Do not insist that he learn the words at this time.

The

couch	crawl
ants	creep
in	and
mouse	go

abode   house

-6-

Line Overlap
    Directions: Ask your child to draw a line under the words overlapping below the line and to mark the extension with an X. Do not insist that he learn these words at this time.

(Part A)

creep   you

ants   crawl

up   spot

    Directions: Now, ask him to draw a line under the words overlapping above the line and mark the extension with an X. He does not need to learn the words at present.

(Part B)

good   day

under   home   see

abode   explore   attic

89

Word Length

Directions: Ask him to draw a line under the long words and 2 lines under the short words in each line. (First, make certain he knows the difference between long and short.) He need not know all of the words at this time.

(long)	and	in	where
	come	mouse	to
	can	Eeka	you
(short)	by	home	is
	your	see	go
	you	out	abode

Unit Form Matching

Directions: Ask your child to draw a line under the words which are the same as the one at the top of each column.

(can)	*(now)*	*(thing)*	*(home)*	*(mouse)*
pan	cow	thing	home	house

90

can	sow	bring	come	mouse
ran	now	sing	home	mouse
fan	how	thing	dome	douse

-9-

Unit Form Context and Matching

Directions: Ask him to draw a line under the word in the sentence which is the same as the first word.

(cats)   We have some cats.

(ran)   He ran home.

(crawl)   Most ants crawl.

(creeps)   Eeka creeps to her home.

(explored)   We explored the attic today.

(are)   J and P are ants.

(mouse)   Eeka is a mouse.

10

Unit Form Phrase Matching

Directions: Ask your child to underline the phrase which coincides with the phrase on the left.

to walk   Ritz likes to walk.

a house   Warmwood is a house.

Eeka walked   Eeka walked to the attic door.

Saw a jar   J and P saw a jar.

the house   How warm the house is.

Unit Form Picture Matching

Directions: Provide a picture of the object given on the left side of the page. Print three sentences containing words beginning with the same first letter as the picture name on the right side of each page, and then ask him to match the appropriate sentence to each picture.

picture of a bird   This is a bear.

                                           This is a bird.

                                           This is a bunny.

picture of a mouse	This is a mouse.
	This is a monster.
	This is a melon.
picture of a boy	This is a boy.
	This is a bear.
	This is a bird.
picture of a dog	This is a duck.
	This is a dime.
	This is a dog.
picture of a house	This is a house.
	This is a hand.
	This is a heart.

-12-

Matching

Directions: Print a word on a piece of very thin paper. Then, ask your child to match this word to a word in a sentence by having him move the thin paper over the sentence until it is directly over the matched word.

Unit Form Configuration

Directions: Ask your child to place a mark under the word that matches the picture you provide.

abode	dog
mouse	house
woods	ants
door	attic
case	couch

Word Acting

Directions: Make short sentences which he can act out by using words such as the following:

in	big
under	small
soft	Eeka
beside	hard

good	sour
above	sweet
laugh	stand
cry	sit
happy	walk
sad	run
over	hop
beyond	creep
none	hot
low	cold

-15-

Form Closure

Directions: Say: "Carefully read the page. Then, without looking up, underline the word that correctly finishes each sentence."

Sample

Ritz walked to the couch. He said, "Good day, Spot." He ran upstairs. He saw Eeka.

Ritz walked to the _____
(couch, creep,)

_____ said, "Good day, Spot."
(She, he, they)

He _____ upstairs.
(walked, talked, ran)

He _____ Eeka.
(saw, was, said)

-16-

Context Identification
   Directions: Ask your child to tell you the correct word in each sentence.

Eeka is a mouse.
             house.

Ritz is a boy.
          toy.

Spot is a dog.
          hog.

J and P are ants.
            pants.

Spot sleeps under the couch.
                    pouch.

-17-

Unit Form Framing

Directions: Pronounce one of the words in each line and then ask your child to point to it and say it.

are	is	look	a	ran
I	walk	creep	your	run
you	crawl	jar	come	water

Exercise Model 17 is the last one given for this approach. Remember, you will be referred to these exercise models in the First Phase Reader. In order to teach certain pages in the First Phase Reader, you will be requested to utilize and at times, to construct exercises similar to those just given. When you are asked to construct an exercise on your own, an appropriate exercise model number will be given for you to use as a pattern.

Now that you have carefully read and studied this teaching emphasis, you will need to write a brief summary of it in the space provided on your child's personal Generic-History-Observation Form. When you have done this and are satisfied, read the Trial Teaching example and then turn to the First Phase Reader Section.

TEACHING APPROACH EMPHASIS II

Sound Syntax

The rationale for this emphasis was drawn largely from the works of Cordts, Robinson, Durrell, and Strickland. Your first task in using this emphasis is to make certain your child knows the twenty-six letters of the alphabet by name, as well as some of the individual letter sounds. Since you are presently studying this emphasis, your child's history-observation and Scores Profile have indicated that he has a limited degree of mastery in this area. (Model exercises for this kind of review are provided for in later pages of this section.)

Once he has become proficient in naming individual letters, you need to approach the introduction of initial or beginning word sounds in the following manner. During the first few teaching sessions, print the name of your child beneath his picture and mount it on a card. This will help him to relate his own picture with his name. Emphasis should then be placed on the first sound heard when the name is pronounced. Ask your child to point to the first letter sound heard in his name when he pronounces it. This will not be difficult for children whose names begin with single initial sounds such as: Terry, Martha, and Kimberly. However, you will have to explain to your child, if he is named Sheila or Charles, for example, that a combination of two letter sounds forms the initial sound in the name.

After he has achieved a facility in learning to identify the initial sound of his name, he is to proceed to other initial sounds including First Phase Reader story character names and neighborhood friends. In selecting names of friends, choose those most useful to the learning of initial sounds, that is, names beginning with single consonant sounds such as Carl, Mary, Bob, Pete, etc. Since he knows these children by their first names, he should have little trouble in this context. Here, it is important to select only *some* of the names, so that valuable time will not be lost trying to explain the more complicated letter combination sounds which inevitably begin some of their names.

After he has become familiar with several initial letter sounds, print the letters on three by five index cards and ask him to pronounce those letters. In conducting this activity, tell him to think of one of the letter sounds and then try to think of another word with the same initial sound. Be very careful here, not to suggest any examples, for he will probably then only respond with those words you give him.

It will probably be necessary for you to select the words from those suggested to be used. Though you should not give examples, you can drop hints of words that would be suitable for him to say. For example, when looking for an "M" word you might say, "Think of the word that tells what a grown up boy is," or "Father is a ————" obviously asking for the word "man."

Through use of this technique, your child can form a list of words that you can keep which have similar initial sounds. Move from this list of words back to review of the initial sounds of the friends' names. One way to do this, would be to line up all of the words and point to a "b" sound, for example. Repeat this activity several times until he begins to know them.

Each time you introduce a new sound, review the sounds your child has already had. Everyone knows how quickly we forget things if we don't use them very much. The same is true in reading. Until the use of the sounds becomes a habit, you and he must practice and practice. After the first sound is taught talk about another beginning consonant sound. Take, for instance, the letter *D*. You might ask him to name all the things in the house that begin with the letter *D* (or whatever sound you choose). After he understands what the *D* sound is like, you can mix up the words beginning with sounds he has already learned and ask which ones begin with the *D* sound and which ones begin with other sounds already taught.

The remaining beginning consonant sounds may be taught in the same way. As your child sees the same word many times, he will be able to identify the whole word, not just the beginning sound. As he continues, he will notice that the words he uses also end with sounds he knows. For example, after he learns the sound that the letters *b* and *d* make, he will remember that the word bird begins with the *b* sound and that it ends with the *d* sound.

Sometimes, two consonants blending in a specific way begin a word, as in tree, black, crayon, etc. Hence, he comes to learn that a blend of two sounds provides a new beginning consonant sound made up of two individual consonant sounds he already knows. You can teach your child these new beginning sounds in the same fashion you taught the beginning consonant sounds of one letter. For instance, you may tell him to find two letters which, when sounded together, begin a word you give him.

As he learns the sounds of the letters in the alphabet, review them many times. If you continue in this fashion, his word attack skill will gradually increase to the point that he will know the word just by looking at it, without even having to think first what the beginning sound is.

This is all much less complicated than it sounds, because you will have been following the procedures outlined in the First Phase Reader, so that sounding skills your child has been acquiring are used to learn the words given in the reader.

Once he has become relatively familiar with consonant sounds, you should turn to the vowel sounds. In teaching him these sounds, you need to begin by reviewing the letter names of the vowels a, e, i, o, u, and sometimes w and y. After this review, move to the short sounds of vowels by using the following key: the short *a* as in apple, the short *e* as in elephant, the short *i* as in Indian, the short *o* as in octopus, and the short *u* as in uncle.

Teach the short *a* sound first by asking him to tell you as many words as he can which begin with this vowel sound. While he gives them to you, write them on a piece of paper and, with each word, ask him to "read" it and say whether it really does have a short *a* sound. (As each new word is "read" you can also review their consonant sounds.) When he knows the short *a* sound relatively well, move to the remaining short vowel sounds in the order given above.

Once he has practiced the short vowels, proceed to the long vowels and teach him those. Teach these in the same fashion you taught the short vowels, after reminding him that a long vowel simply says its own name. (For example, you should write words beginning with the long *a* as in *ape*). Continue with the other long vowels, presenting one a day, until he learns them. After the long *a*, go to the long *e* as in *evening*; the long *i* as in *ice*; the long *o* as in *oats*; and the long *u* as in *uke*. Then, review the long and short vowel sounds with him and give additional practice by using words that have the vowel in the middle of the word.

As he comes to learn the different sounds in our language, he will begin to notice that one letter can stand for more than one sound (as in the letter *c*). He will learn that when two vowels come together, they make a special sound and he will notice that many words end with the silent letter *e*. As he begins to read, he will learn these sounding characteristics and many more. However, he will not learn all of them in the First Phase Reader. Indeed, all through his later school years and throughout his adult life, he will continously learn new things about the sounds in our language.

As your child reads along in the First Phase Reader, he will obviously encounter words both new and strange to him. Since he doesn't yet read well enough to use the dictionary, he must learn to read these words on his own. He will be able to do this, if you have taught him according to the preceding outline, because he will have developed the "know how" to independently look at letters or groups of letters in a given word by asking and resolving a number of questions: What is the beginning sound? What is the ending sound? Are the letters in the middle familiar? If so, what are their sounds? This independently based skill will enable him to put the sounds together, starting with the beginning sound, in a logical and meaningful fashion.

Now that you have completed reading the description of the Sound Syntax Teaching Approach Emphasis, you are ready to look at some ways to implement it. The following section is to be read and used in conjunction with this emphasis in the First Phase Reader. However, for the present, you are asked to carefully read the following Exercise Models and to refer to the first part of this approach description when a question arises.

101

Sound Syntax Exercise Models

Please recall that these exercises are to be used as given or as models for you to use in constructing similar exercises when, and as, you are requested to use them in the teaching portion of the First Phase Reader. Please, provide for approximately thirty minute sessions for each of these and similar exercises.

-1-

Alphabet Name Review I

Directions: On a standard sized piece of paper, print the letters of the alphabet, five to a line with the "Z" occupying a line by itself. While printing the letters, have the child by your side and ask him to help you in any way he can. In writing the letters, write each letter in its capital form, immediately followed by its lower case form. For example: A, a; B, b; C, c; D, d; E, e; F, f; G, g; H, h; I, i; J, j; K, k; L, l; and so forth. As you and he print them, name them and see if he can name them, too. Remember, knowing the correct order of letters is not important at this time. If you have an alphabet book, you may use this, to help him review and learn the letters and their names.

-2-

Alphabet Name Review II

Directions: Place each of the twenty-six letters of the alphabet on a separate card and work with him using each card, until he knows both their capital and lower case forms by name. Be certain to mix the order of the cards from time to time, so that he will not merely memorize their order of presentation. Continue this exercise periodically, two or three times a week, until he becomes quite proficient in letter name knowledge.

Picture Naming — Sounding I

Directions: Carefully print your child's first name under a photograph of him mounted on a card or sheet of paper. Do the same, if you can, with some of his friends and family members' photographs. Then, ask him to give you the name of the first letter and its sound in each name. In obtaining names, try to get those that *begin with a single consonant sound.* (In helping him sound these initial letters, you may need to refer to the sounding chart given as Model Exercise 15.)

Picture Naming — Sounding II

Directions: Using each picture in the First Phase Reader as you get to them, and when requested by the First Phase Reader, ask your child to name as many picture details as he can. List the details by name, on a sheet of paper, and have him give you as many of the beginning sounds of the details as possible.

Consonant Naming — Sounding I

Directions: Each time you introduce a new initial letter sound by using a word given in the First Phase Reader, be sure to review the sounds he has already learned. Do this by keeping the cards containing the letter sounds, so you can go over them with him for the photographs and reader. The order in which you introduce these initial sounds depends on the pictures you have used and on the order of word presentation given in the First Phase Reader.

Consonant Naming — Sounding II

Directions: Print two letters on separate cards, with which he is familiar with respect to their sounds and ask him to pronounce these letters and their sounds. Then, ask him to think of words beginning with these same two sounds. Write the words on a sheet of paper as he gives them to you. When he is finished, go over with him each of the words he gave you, discuss them, and keep them for later review.

Naming — Sounding III

Directions: Repeat Exercise Models 5 and 6, only this time work with the ending sounds of letters, using words from the photographs and First Phase Reader pictures and words.

Sounding Consonant Letter Combinations

Directions: Some of the words appearing in the First Phase reader begin with consonant blends. That is, two consonants appear together to make a sound unique, in that neither of the two consonants taken alone make the same sound as when they appear together. You will be referred to this Exercise Model when this occurs in the First Phase Reader. Teach these blends in the same fashion as you have taught individual consonant sounds, as outlined in exercise models five and six. Be sure to explain to him that when certain letter combinations appear, they make new sounds unlike sounds they make when they appear alone. (Exercise Model 14 will help you here, since it is a chart of all of the consonant blends he will need.)

Short Vowel Naming — Sounding I

Directions: Review the letter names of the vowels with him . . . a, e, i, o, u, and sometimes Y. Then, present him with the following key words, while telling him that these make particular sounds called short sounds, as follows: *a* as in apple; *e* as in elephant; *i* as in Indian; *o* as in octopus; and *u* as in uncle. Present these together and then ask him if he can think of other words beginning with these sounds.

Short Vowel Naming — Sounding II

Directions: Continue with Exercise Model 9 until he begins to get a grasp of the sounds, then follow the same procedure for the short vowels as they appear in the middle of words. Here, you can give key words such as *cat, bed, cot*, and *cut*.

Long Vowels Naming — Sounding

Directions: Follow the same procedures given in Exercise Models nine and ten for the long vowels. Tell him that long vowels simply say their own names. Here you can use key words such as *ape, cape; evening, leap; ice; bite; oats, coats; uke, cute*, etc. If he notices that a word ending in *e*, usually gives the middle vowel the long sound, fine, but do not dwell on it. You will not need to spend as much time on this, as you did on the short vowels.

12

Total Sounding

Directions: Use this exercise when you are asked to, in the teaching portion of the First Phase Reader, in the following manner. Whenever a new word is introduced in the reader, you are to teach it to your child by first pronouncing the word; secondly, asking him to pronounce it; thirdly, putting the word on a separate sheet of paper or card; fourthly, asking him to give you the beginning sound; fifthly, asking him to give you the ending sound; sixthly, asking him to give you the letter name and each individual sound in the word; seventhly, asking him to pronounce the word again, and finally, having him discuss the meaning of the word with you.

-13-

General Review

Directions: As you proceed through the First Phase Reader, periodically review the word lists you have been compiling as a result of the exercises. The general idea here, is to encourage self-seeking on the part of your child by teaching him to question each word in terms of its beginning, ending and medial sounds and its meaning.

-14-

Consonant Blend Chart

Directions: Use this chart as a key, as you need it. Encourage your child to produce other words using these blend or letter combinations.

Th— Draw a sketch of a thimble (it is the first sound you hear)
the, there, that, them,

Wh— Draw a sketch of a wheel (it is the first sound you hear)
when, what, whee, where, wham

Ch— Draw a sketch of a chair (it is the first sound you hear)
chap, choose, champ, chimp, chip

Sh— Draw a sketch of a ship (it is the first sound you hear)
shirt, shall, show, sheep, shoot

The other less common consonant blends are given in the First Phase Reader as they appear. The above represents the general procedure you will follow in teaching them.

-15-

Consonant Letter Sounding Key

Directions: Using the following for a key, you and your child finish developing the chart, by reproducing it on separate pieces of paper and sketching in the drawings requested. Have your child do as much of this as possible, when you are asked to do so, in the First Phase Reader.

			drawing		*drawing*
B or b	–	bed		cab	
C or c	–	cat		*	
D or d	–	dog		bed	
F or f	–	fish		golf	

G or g	–	game	pig
H or h	–	house	*
J or j	–	jungle	*
K or k	–	keg	duck
L or l	–	lamp	seal
M or m	–	mouse	dam
N or n	–	noose	in
P or p	–	paper	map
Q or q (kw)	–	queen	*
R or r	–	rat	fur*
S or s	–	sail	boss
T or t	–	top	boat
V or v	–	vase	*
W or w	–	woods	*
X or x	–	axe*	fox*
Y or y	–	yard	*
Z or z	–	zebra	fuzz

Those words which have been designated by an asterisk (*), are those which seldom end in the letters marked, or their sounds are changed, depending upon their position in words. Therefore, at this time, do not stress their teaching as these special cases are provided for, as the need arises, in the First Phase Reader.

Exercise Model 15 is the last one given for this approach. You will be referred to these models in the First Phase Reader. In order to teach certain pages in the reader, you will be asked to construct and use exercises similar to those just given. When you are requested to do this, an appropriate exercise model number will be given for you to use as a pattern.

You realize, of course, that all of the sounding patterns were not given. Do not worry, your child will be learning these patterns for the rest of his life. Exceptions and omissions are handled by the First Phase Reader so that he can learn to read, and read well, with this approach.

Now that you have carefully read and studied this teaching approach, you need to write a brief summary of it in the space provided on your child's personal Generic History-Observation Form. When you have finished this task, and are satisfied as to your knowledge of this approach, read the Trial Teaching Example and then turn to the First Phase Reader Section.

Should you not seem to be achieving the success you and your child feel you should when you have worked with this approach for some time, do not despair, for this has been considered in the construction of the First Phase Reader. Should this situation occur, you will be referred back to this section at the appropriate time in the reader. If this indeed does materialize, begin again with the first page of the First Phase Reader, only this time using the Visual-Motor-Touch Teaching Approach Emphasis.

TEACHING APPROACH EMPHASIS III

Visual-Motor-Touch

The rationale for this emphasis was drawn largely from the works of Fernald and Montessori. According to Fernald, certain perceptual and motor skills must be mastered by the child before learning to read. Skills which help him to "see an object in space" and differentiate between it and its surroundings must be tied to the ability to control the muscles which affect visual, kinesthetic (movement), and tactile (touch) perception of the object in the reading process.

The actual process of learning to read is adapted in an effort to make reading both interesting and more concrete to the young child. Since it is thought that he learns by manipulating his environment and by investigating those things which arouse his curiosity, a method is needed which makes it possible for the child to learn to read by taking part in structured activities based upon his own desires and interests. This, of course, represents a studied endeavor to make education relevant to the child, while still providing him with necessary reading skills.

In most reading methods, only one sense is utilized, so that the child who has difficulty differentiating among letters using vision alone may be greatly hampered. Since your child's Scores Profile indicated that he can benefit most from a multi-sensory approach, you are going to use as many of the senses as possible in teaching him to read. In this regard, the tactile or touch aspect is quite important − in that, if necessary, he can literally "feel" a word he needs to read.

Ideally, your child should not be forced to learn anything he has not evidenced some interest in. However, this is not to say that you are to let him completely alone in these areas that he does not express interest. You must develop his interests through stimulating materials, in the case of reading, through proper use of the First Phase Reader. Your job in teaching the First Phase Reader vocabulary, then, is to help him first of all, to develop a desire to learn the words presented.

In order to derive benefit from Visual-Motor-Touch Teaching Emphasis your child must have structured experiences in large and small muscle control. This is accomplished in the Exercise Model section of this emphasis through the presentation of activities intended to develop a comprehensive knowledge of his bodily parts and their arrangements with respect to one another. In addition, he needs experiences which will enhance his ability to tell differences among visual objects. These too, are provided for in the Exercise Model section.

The general procedure you will use in teaching the First Phase Reader is as follows: You will introduce a word from the reader by discussing it in a way designed to interest him in it. You then print the word for him on a piece of paper, after having described each letter in the word and the sound each usually represents, so that he will get the idea that those strange symbols on the paper do have meaning. (It is necessary that he have some understanding of what sounds the letters usually stand for if he is going to be able to figure out new words later on in the reader. It is very important, however, to emphasize that *the sound of the whole word is much more significant* than the individual sound of each letter.)

Your child then takes the paper with the word printed on it and traces over the letters with his index finger. (As he traces, you need to emphasize the importance of always moving from the left to the right when reading and writing). He continues this finger tracing until he feels relatively certain he knows the movements involved in writing this particular word. At that time, the word is covered and he tries to write it on his own, from memory. Covering the paper and asking him to use his memory is important; otherwise he could simply copy the various patterns of lines that make up your printed model and not learn exactly how the word is written.

When he begins to write the word from memory, ask him to say it. Try to get him to synchronize the speaking and the writing of the word, so they end at about the same time. But remember, you do not want him to pronounce each letter sound of the word separately. In other words, if for example, he is writing the word "dog," he should not be permitted to say "duh-o-guh". You should tell him to think of the individual letter sounds, but not to say them, because letters hardly ever stand by themselves. The important thing is the sound they make when they are together with other letters to make a word.

After mastering the words in this way, on the first page or two of the First Phase Reader, encourage their use in some kind of meaningful context by suggesting that he retell or make up a new story with the words. Do not expect the first few stories to be more than one or two sentences long. In time, they will become more complex.

When he tells you these first stories write them down to give them back to him to read. Later, after he acquires some writing proficiency and a larger vocabulary, he may write his own. The creating of his own reading material will help him become a more proficient reader and develop a deeper interest and appreciation for books in general.

In varying the word learning using this emphasis, you will want to include activities involving rhythm, drawing, acting, and body portrayal. These types of activities are also provided for you in the Exercise Model section. The main idea is to totally involve the whole child in learning to read, by making use of all of his senses, in as many concrete ways as possible.

Once your child begins to write sentences with his newly learned words, explain the difference between capitalized and uncapitalized letters. You need to provide practice adequate enough in this, so that your child will become faimiliar with both forms of all letters. The teaching of the capitalized letters is accomplished in the same fashion as the teaching of the new words. (Exercise Models are given for this activity.)

In time he will become so skilled at learning new words, that fewer and fewer tracings will be necessary before he can write the words on his own, and eventually the tracing phase can be eliminated all together. At this time, ask him to form a mental image of it, then attempt to write it from memory. If he seems unable to do this for any given word, the word he wrote should be compared to your model with a discussion as to how they differ. After doing this, ask him to try writing the word again from memory. If he still cannot do it, go back to the tracing phase for awhile.

Once he is able to learn words by simply looking at them, being told what they are, pronouncing them once or twice, and writing them for memory; he should be helped to develop some sophisticated reading skills such as: attending details and their interrelationships; story relating in terms of his own direct or vicariously acquired experiential background; identifying emotional reactions and story character motivation; developing visual imagery from written descriptions; and predicting outcomes and making inferences.

Dramatizing the stories that are read should be especially emphasized at this point, because this will be of considerable aid in developing comprehension skills. If you ask him to act out a story, he will certainly have to note details and the relationships between them, interpret the story, be able to show the emotions and motives of the story characters, form mental images, and predict the outcome. Here, you must provide opportunity for free movement so that a variety of interpretations is possible.

In time, your child will acquire the skill to learn new reading words independently by simply noting similarities between them and those he already knows. This will enable you to place primary emphasis on the further development and refinement of comprehension skills.

Now that you have finished reading the description of this emphasis, you are prepared to study some ways of putting it into practice. The following portion is to be read, and later used, with this emphasis and the First Phase Reader. For the present, you are requested to carefully read the following Exercise Models and to refer to the first part of this emphasis description when you have a question.

Please note that these exercises are to be utilized as given, or as models for you to use in constructing similar exercises when, and as, you are asked to use them by the teaching portion of the First Phase Reader. Please provide for approximately thirty minute sessions for each of these and those you construct.

-1-

Large Muscle Control
Directions: Provide plenty of free, clear space and ask your child to perform various physical feats including tumbling, jumping, somersaulting, balancing, head standing, standing at attention, sitting up straight, balancing objects, throwing, catching, running in place, lifting arms, etc. In general, get him to engage in any physical activity or bodily posture you can conceive of and can maintain under your control. The important points are, that you have his activities performance under your leadership and that he understands the physical feats he can accomplish and control, when various parts of his body work together. (Any book containing various physical exercises will be useful with this Exercise Model.)

-2-

Tactile Enhancement
Directions: Place a number of differently textured objects with which your child is unfamiliar, in several different paper bags. Ask him to reach in without looking, select one, handle it, turn his head so he cannot see it, and hand it to you. Than, have him draw or describe what he has just felt, but has not seen.

114

Aural Enhancement

Directions: Assemble a number of different objects which either produce a sound or which you can use to produce a sound. Position your child so that he cannot see you use the objects to produce sound. Use one, then ask him to either reproduce it orally or to describe it. You may also wish to use phonograph records or tapes for this exercise. If you use these you can add to the exercise by having him signal in some fashion to you, changes in volume, speed, pitch, etc.

Aural Tactile Enhancement

Directions: Position the child where he cannot see what you are doing and continue Exercise Models 2 and 3. Specifically, have him handle and make sounds with a number of sound producing objects in a bag. When he is finished you reproduce the sounds with another set of identical objects, one at a time, which he cannot see, and then ask him to reach into the bag, without looking, handle the objects therein, and then hand you the sound making object which is identical to yours.

Body Portrayal

Directions: Ask your child to use his whole body in looking like specific animals, plants, or objects that you name. For example, you may tell him to be a bear, dog, tree, desk, carrot, etc. If he does not understand in the beginning, demonstrate for him.

Small Muscle Control I

Directions: Show him a number of meaningless different one line drawings such as slashes, angles, arcs, etc., cut from sandpaper. Ask him to trace over them one at a time with his index finger until he feels he can reproduce any one of them on paper. Then, let him reproduce the ones he selected on paper without looking.

Small Muscle Control II

Directions: Give him a large sheet of paper on which you have, using the top half, drawn three different geometric symbols such as squares, circles, lines, etc. Ask him to reproduce them, by copying them in, on the lower half of the paper.

8

Letter Introduction

Directions: Cut the lower case letters from sheets of sandpaper so that each letter is about three inches high. Mount these on white index cards, one per card. Introduce the letters, one at a time, by handing him the card and naming the letter and the sound it makes. (You may use Exercise Model 15, in the Sound Syntax Emphasis as a key for the individual letter sounds.) Have him trace any given letter, using his index finger, with his eyes closed, while saying its sound and its name softly, over and over.

Letter Introduction II

Directions: Give him a sheet of paper on which you have written five letters he has previously learned. Ask him to trace over these with a pencil while saying their names and sounds.

Letter Introduction III

Directions: Repeat Exercise Model 8 for capital letters once he has become familiar with them in their small case form.

Word Introduction I

Directions: As words are introduced in the First Phase Reader, follow this procedure *when requested to do so in the Teaching Section:* (1) reproduce each new word on an index card using capital or small case letters as given; (2) give him the index card and pronounce the word; (3) ask him to trace each letter in the word with his index finger thinking of, (but not uttering aloud) each letter sound; (4) when he has finished tracing the entire word, have him pronounce it; and (5) have him print the word from memory on the reverse side of the card.

Word Introduction II

Directions: Discuss the meaning of each new word you introduce, by asking him how he thinks each relates to the illustration and to the story. Let him have the word index cards to refer to while you and he are talking. Be sure to save the cards.

Word and Story Meaning

Directions: After he has learned a number of words, give him the cards with those words and ask him to use them to retell or make up a new story from the First Phase Reader.

117

Word and Story Practice

Directions: By the time you get through approximately the first half of the First Phase Reader, you will probably be able to eliminate the tracing phase given in Exercise Model 11 from the new word introduction. This means that you can give him any new word on a card, pronounce it, discuss its many meanings and have him reproduce it from memory. At this time, you can use Exercise Model 13 in written form when requested by the Teaching Section of the First Phase Reader. That is, he should be able to use his card file to copy various words on paper so as to retell one of the reader stories or make up one of his own.

-15-

Story Dramas

Directions: After reading a given story section, ask him to act it out by taking the role of each of the story characters in turn. You may vary this activity by taking one or more parts of the story yourself.

In using these Exercise Models with this emphasis, it is extremely important for you to note that you *are not particularly interested in how well the child can reproduce the letter symbols in printed form.* The important thing is that they are recognizable. *You are not teaching printing as such.* The printing is a means to an end, that is, that he learn to read. Remember too, that any printing he does, must be done from left to right because he is learning to read from left to right.

-16-

The following, Exercise Model 16, is given to you as a general format to follow in printing letters. It is not to be used pre-scriptively. In printing the letters, begin at the top of each symbol.

When you make an arc or circle as a letter part, do so in a counter-clockwise direction.

For example:$l + o = b$ or p; $o + l = d$ or q;\ $+ / = x$; etc. The important thing to remember here is to use only arcs, circles and straight lines.

In making capital letters, you can follow the same general pattern of arc, circle, and straight line. I have purposely eliminated examples for the capital letters to stress that their painstaking and meticulous reproduction is not the goal here.

Exercise Model 16 is the last one given for this emphasis. Please recall that you will be referred to these Exercise Models by the First Phase Reader. In order to teach certain pages in the reader, you will be requested to use and in time, to construct, these and similar exercises. When you are requested to construct an exercise on your own, you will be referred to an appropriate Exercise Model for use as a pattern.

Now that you have carefully read and studied this teaching emphasis, you will need to write a brief summary of it in the space provided on your Individualized Generic History-Observation Form. When you have summarized this to your satisfaction, read the Trial Teaching Example and then turn to the First Phase Reader Section.

TEACHING APPROACH EMPHASIS IV

Voice Impress-Look Along-Part I

This approach emphasis, unlike the preceding three, is to be used with the Experience Unit Section, not with the First Phase Reader. You will recall that this emphasis is intended to help get the child ready to read in the First Phase Reader. As such, it is more of a preparatory emphasis than a teaching one.

When your child has successfully completed the Gray section which immediately follows the description of this emphasis, you will need to reread this description, especially the second part to determine what you are to do at that time. Please do not become impatient with your child and hurry through the Gray section. The Scores Profile and your own Generic History-Observation have indicated that your child needs a certain type of instruction prior to the formal teaching of reading. If you read and utilize the Gray section very carefully and fairly slowly, you will make the developmental progress necessary for beginning reading instruction. On the other hand, if you rush through it with him, the chances are quite good that you will have wasted both his and your time.

The first step in using this emphasis is to make certain that your child is a "good" listener. This is the heart of this emphasis and the activities found in the Gray section following it. Indeed, you will have won ninety per cent of the game once he becomes an attentive and actively participating listener.

Everyone, except maybe politicians, listen more than they speak or read. Therefore, facility with oral language through listening is a necessary forerunner of reading proficiency.

According to Strickland, children go through a series of stages in the development of their listening ability. At first a young child does very little listening except when he is directly spoken to or is concerned personally with a particular conversational topic. He does not just listen attentively and absorb most, or all, that is being said and done around him. He does, however, learn to listen more as he matures, but he is easily distracted. Later he seems to be listening more, but usually he is only half listening and waiting to present his own pure ideas. In short, he is hearing, but he is not doing anything constructive with what he is hearing.

This is where you come in. "Good" listening can be brought about by careful labor on your part. By dint or great effort, you can transform your child into a critical listener through noting when your child listens and what he likes to listen to.

Before any good teaching can take place, the home atmosphere must be conducive to listening. This is extremely important since it can affect the whole course and purpose of what you are trying to do. In fact, preparing for the best listening possible will make your child ready for listening. Regardless of the effectiveness of the techniques you are using, if he does not want to listen, he will not. The home atmosphere should be relaxed, comfortable and as informal as possible. Distractions in the form of extraneous noise, such as street traffic and neighborhood activities, should be eliminated if possible. You and your child should be quite comfortable and so positioned that you can see and interact with one another without difficulty. Your child is much more likely to listen to you if he is facing you and is comfortable.

In beginning to teach your child how to listen, you will need to use many sound experiences within his home environment. You and he should discuss the various sound sources within the home, in an effort to help him come to realize that listening can be done anywhere and at anytime. Your child needs to develop an awareness of all these sounds, and after listening, be able to discuss what he has heard. This practice in relating what he has heard will later be transferred to telling what he has read.

According to Dawson, there are two important necessities for listening as a basis for reading. First, your child needs to be able to tell differences among sounds and secondly, he must be able to listen for specific purposes. If he can successfully develop these skills, he will be taking a big step toward good listening and, therefore, good reading.

Research tells us that the first listening activities should be designed to help the child to notice the difference between sounds that are not similar. For example, the child should realize that running down a walk sounds differently than someone hammering a nail. Have your child talk about the kinds of sounds that he hears everyday. Discuss the sounds heard in the home, and outside with him. Help him to think of ways that sounds are similar or different. After he has had a chance to think about different sounds, ask him to imitate some of them. This can be done, either with his own voice or with the aid of a physical device in the room which might be handy.

In learning to identify sounds it is necessary to be able to tell what makes them sound differently. So, he must learn to tell if a sound is loud or soft, high or low, rough or smooth, and pleasant or unpleasant. This is important for him to know, since sometimes the meaning of a word or sentence depends on how an individual says it.

After mastering this, you need to discuss how people raise and lower their voices when speaking. A good deal of time should be spent on this phase since you are attempting to relate the spoken word to the written word. You can begin by discussing how his voice sounds when he says something, when he asks something, or when he commands something. After discussing these various ways of speaking, you can give your child a sentence — a very simple sentence — and ask him to say it in three different modes.

According to Durrell, the most important aspect of becoming a good listener is to be able to hear the differences in words and letters. So you can sound out individual letters and have your child repeat each letter after you. You can also talk about how the mouth is shaped and where the tongue is located when the sound is made. In doing this, ask him to feel the shape of his mouth as he makes each sound and to repeat each sound several times. (You need to listen carefully to be sure that he is making each sound correctly.) Then you can move on to repeating nonsense syllables. (The nonsense exercises should include syllables beginning with all the different consonants. You may wish to refer to Exercise Models 9, 11, and 15 in the Sound Syntax Emphasis if you need a Sounding Key.)

In teaching your child how to listen to parts of words and how to put these parts together to make words, write the syllable being repeated on a piece of paper where he can see it as he repeats it. When teaching this aspect of listening, you need not go into the differences among written letters but present them along with the sound and permit the child to absorb the letters as he typically absorbs other things.

Various reading experts, including Smith and Hester, tell us that listening for a purpose is as important for future reading as learning to discriminate among sounds. If a child can not listen for a purpose, he will be unable to read to get the central thought or important details. He will read word by word and attach no meaning to what

122

any given combination of words has produced. Again, at this point, it might help to explain that reading is like talking. Your child does not just listen to individual words but understands purposes and meanings of combinations of words. He makes use of verbal intonations which he must transfer to future reading. He needs to learn to listen purposefully, accurately, and critically in order to be able to read in a similar fashion.

There are different areas involved in learning to listen for a purpose, and various activities are presented in the Gray section for teaching the child in these areas. First, he must learn to listen for the central thought, idea, or purpose of a story. He must also be taught to listen for specific details found within a story. Another important aspect of listening for a purpose is developing the ability to remember facts or sequential order.

In order to read the child must be able to draw inferences and develop conclusions from what he has read. This is first developed through listening. A story can be told or read until a critical point, and then he can be asked to tell what he thinks will happen or to draw a picture of the ending he anticipates.

Classifying objects is another important listening and reading skill which can be taught by having your child put furniture, toys, or people in correct places after hearing a story.

All of the preceding listening skills are significant. Mastery of them, on the part of your child, will enable him to undertake beginning reading instruction with every potential chance for success. In other words, the better he masters these listening skills, the better his chances for mastery of future reading skills.

Voice Impress-Look Along-Part II (after finishing the Gray section)

Once he has become proficient in the listening skills and you have finished the Gray section, you are ready to use the final step in this approach emphasis. It is from this final step that the emphasis draws its name, that is, the Voice Impress-Look Along. For this is exactly what you and your child do.

Here is how you go about it: Go to the public library, neighborhood school, or bookstore and obtain several children's storybooks on a first grade level. Be certain to get books with which your child is unfamiliar. Take him with you, if at all possible, so that he can choose for himself from a number you have designated that are on the first grade level. Let him, if the budget can stand it, select four or five. Remember here, the thicker the book the better and the fewer pictures and more words, the better.

Now, at this point, some bad news, maybe. You will need thirty-five or forty books before you are finished. So the more you can borrow, the more healthy your budget remains. Ask your neighbor for books if you can, but do not obtain books higher than a first grade level.

In using this emphasis, do not permit your child to "read" the books before you use them with him. That is, at the most, let him look them over very briefly if he wants, but do not go beyond this.

When you and your child are ready, select one of the books he is especially excited about and sit down with him in such a position that both you and he can see the book's pages easily and conveniently. Then, tell him that you are going to read the story to him, *using a card to uncover each line* (not word) as you read and that you want him to "read" along with you using just his eyes for this time.

Tell him that you intend to read every page twice and that during the second reading of the page, you would like for him to read aloud with you, after you have discussed what you read on the first reading. (During the discussion after your initial reading, be sure to talk about any illustrations appearing on that page.)

Got the picture? This is the manner in which you are to proceed through all thirty-five or forty books. Do not read too fast, be sure you use the card on both the first and second readings, allow plenty of time for discussion, use the page's pictures in the discussion and do not expect him to "read" aloud perfectly or right with you. In most cases, until the child gets acclimated to the procedure, he will be slightly behind you during your second reading.

124

When you have finished a book, give it to him and let him "read" it to his heart's content. If you and he have the time and inclination, follow this procedure every week day at the same hour for approximately twenty minutes. Remember, you are not in a hurry. From time to time, you may want to return to the Gray section for review, in lieu of a reading session. If your child's interest begins to flag, don't pester him, relax and take a week or two off.

When your child gets to the point that he begins to consistently read somewhat ahead of you, on the second reading and when he can pick out a few words and remember them, continue for a week or so and then go to Approach Emphasis III, Visual-Motor-Touch in the Blue section. Read it carefully, write a short summary of it without referring to the pages containing its description, read the Trial Teaching Example and then begin using Visual-Motor-Touch approach with the First Phase Reader in the Gold section.

VOICE IMPRESS-LOOK ALONG ACTIVITIES AND EXERCISES FOR PART I

The Experiences Unit Section

Here are the two activity series you should use *as the first part of the Voice-Impress Look-Along Teaching Approach Emphasis.* Each series is intended to develop specific listening skills and is placed in a developmental order. That is, you should use these with your child in the order they are presented in this book.

Please do not rush through these. An approximate time allotment is given for each activity based on a daily twenty minute session. However, you may want to spend more time than the number of twenty minute sessions indicated for each.

If your child does not appear particularly interested in these after you start them, quit, while you and he both are ahead of the game and come back to them at a later time. *Plan on at least six months to complete the two activity series.*

Activity One Series

Use this series first. There are five activities in this series, *to be used at the rate of one twenty minute session per week for each activity for at least twelve weeks.*

Activity One A (every Monday)

The procedure for this activity involves you selecting a paragraph from some source and reading it to your child. The objective is to discuss the different sounds that are indicated in it. You read it aloud once, emphasizing the paragraph portions where sounds are made and you then reread it aloud, asking him to make the appropriate sounds when they are indicated. Be certain to pause where sounds are indicated, to give him time to make them.

A sample paragraph is provided below for you to use as the first one. This means you need to find eleven more of them on your own.

(In obtaining the paragraphs, the important thing to keep in mind is their interest level for the child. Therefore, you need not be concerned with the paragraph difficulty level.)

Sample Paragraph

Joe slowly walked over the crunchy leaves. (sound). He was trying to sneak up to the pond in the middle of the woods. As he walked quietly along, he tripped over a dead tree branch. (sound). He pushed himself up and stood very still, hoping that any animals around the pond had not heard him. He finally got to where he could see the pond. There, taking a drink of water was a deer and sitting beside the deer, on a rock, was a frog. Joe slowly raised the camera he had been carrying and snapped the shutter. (sound). At this sound the frog jumped into the water. (sound). The deer leaped away into the forest.

Activity one B (every Tuesday)

Obtain a new coloring book for your child. From this, select a picture and present it along with a word which rhymes with some detail in the picture. Then, ask him to color the picture part which rhymes with the word you said to him. Try to produce three rhyming words for each picture. After he has colored the appropriate picture details, complete the twenty minute session by asking him to finish coloring the whole picture.

Activity one C (every Wednesday)

Get a book of Mother Goose Nursery Rhymes. Read a rhyme to your child and then ask him to draw a picture telling the rhyme. When he has finished, discuss the drawing in detail with him. Begin by asking him how his drawing tells the rhyme you have read. After the discussion, read the rhyme to him again to finish the twenty minute session.

127

Activity one D (every Thursday)

You say two words clearly and distinctly. If the pair of words has the same beginning sound, your child is to clap. If the pair is different, he is to sit silently.

A variation of this is to say three words, only two of which, begin with the same sound. Give your child a chance to say the word in each group that does not begin with the same sound as the other two. Continue this for about ten minutes, then ask him to choose an animal to imitate. First, let him imitate the sound the animal makes. Then ask him to make the sounds of his animal when it is angry, sad, happy, scared, sleepy, etc. Continue this activity for the last ten minutes of this session.

If after a few weeks, he has exhausted his supply of animals, teach him some new ones and continue in the same manner.

Activity one E (every Friday)

For the first five minutes ask your child to stand and follow a list of directions you give him all at once. Example: Walk 3 steps forward, go put your thumb on the left side of the window, say the first 3 letters of the alphabet, and then walk to your chair passing by the door. The child may not proceed until he has heard all directions and none will be repeated to him.

For the remaining fifteen minutes, present a set of directions for a simple paper construction only once and have him carry out its construction. The results will show how much meaningful listening took place.

Activity Two Series

Use this series next. Like the first series, there are five activities included to be used at the rate of *one activity per day for about twenty minutes each time for at least twelve weeks.* In other words, as in the previous series you will repeat each activity at least twelve times.

Activity Two A (every Monday)

Read a part of a short story not heard before to your child and then ask him to finish it in any way he wishes, but insist that he complete it on the basis of what he has heard. When he has finished, discuss his ending with him and then finish reading the story. After doing this, discuss the difference between his ending and the author's. Take about twenty minutes for the entire session.

Activity Two B (every Tuesday)

Give your child two spoons to use as rhythm instruments. Have him practice a simple rhythm such as one long beat, two short, and one long. Then give him two nonsense syllables of the same type. That is, both syllables should begin with a vowel, a consonant or a consonant blend. Let him practice saying the two syllables to the rhythm and then have him beat his "rhythm sticks" and repeat the syllables at the same time.

Example:

Rhythm: Two short, one long, two long
Syllables: ma, ma, me, me, me.
Rhythm with syllables: ma, ma. me, me, me.

Vary the syllables and the rhythm and as he becomes more proficient, add one or two more nonsense syllables. After he has had some practice in hearing different kinds of syllables, further vary the activity by saying a syllable such as "ten" and then asking him to give a syllable which begins with the letter "t." Again, all of the syllables should be of one type. That is, they should all begin with the same consonant.

It is not necessary for you to use the term, "syllable" with your child. He will get the idea without you calling it by its name. (A syllable is a speech sound with one vowel in it.)

Activity Two C (every Wednesday)

This twenty minute session is intended to further develop your child's ear discrimination at a more sophisticated level.

Select any two consonants (any letter of the alphabet other than a, e, i, o, u, w, and y, these are vowels) and make a list of five words beginning with each of your selected consonants and five words ending in your selected consonants. Say them one at a time, pausing after each one and asking him to give you a word beginning with that sound. Repeat this procedure with the five words you selected which end with the same consonant. Then, repeat the same procedure for the other consonant you selected.

During each weekly session thereafter, review the previous week's consonant for the first five minutes and add two more. Continue this procedure until he can give you words, either beginning or ending, with any consonant you indicate. Encourage him to give you different words as beginning or ending consonant examples.

Activity Two D (every Thursday)

During this weekly twenty minute session you are asked to use the same consonants you use on every Wednesday and in the same manner with one modification. Instead of making the activity all oral, put the words you are using to teach beginning and ending consonant sounds on separate sheets of paper.

For example, say one of the consonant sounds you are teaching is the *"b."* Then you could have the following ten words *ball, bat, bait, berry, baby, cob, bib, sob, rub,* and *tub*, each on a separate sheet of paper. (You would also have ten other words for the other consonant sound.) Then, at a table, place the card with "cob" on one side and "bat" on the other side of the table and then tell him you are going

130

to say the word with the beginning or ending sound of "b." (Show him on another piece of paper what "b" looks like.) Then, tell him you want him to point to the word that begins or ends with the sound "b" makes. For example, if you say "cob" he should point to that word since the "b" sound is heard at the end of that word.

Do not become impatient with him. Take your time. Many children require a great deal of exercise with this activity. After he catches on, continue in this fashion until he has mastered the consonant sounds and can tell one consonant from another by looking at it.

Activity Two E (every Friday)

During this weekly twenty minute session, your child is to tell you a story or stories he has heard or composed himself. Initially, you may have to encourage or prompt him to do this by telling him in a sentence or two, something about a topic you know he is quite interested in.

Do not rush him in his stories. If they are quite short, do not be concerned for they will become longer. If you experience undue difficulty with this, simply ask him to tell you in his own words a story you read to him.

Once you and your child have successfully completed this second series of activities, proceed to the Voice-Impress-Look Along Approach Emphasis Part II. You will need to again refer to that section to refresh your memory.

Remember, you are to continue with Part II of this emphasis, using the first grade story books you have obtained, until he begins to "read" ahead of you and begins to pick out words from the text and say them to you. You may then go to Approach Emphasis III, Visual-Motor-Touch, in the Blue section. This is the emphasis you will use in teaching your child the First Phase Reader. Read this emphasis description carefully, write a short summary of it on the individualized Generic History Observation Form from memory, read the Trial Teaching Example and then turn to the Gold section and begin teaching.

Trial Teaching Example

Now that you have completed the reading and study of the approach emphasis you selected to use with your child, please carefully read the following Trial Teaching Example. The following Generic History Observation, teaching approach selection, and sample reading lessons represent an actual child-parent learning-teaching situation. It is presented as a final study task prior to the actual initiation of reading instruction and is intended to demonstrate in outline form, the general use of this book.

Generic History-Observation Outline and Teaching Approach

Ria is the only child of older parents. Her father is well respected in the community and financially well set. Both parents have college educations and Ria's father has done graduate work as well. Ria is a kind little girl and is usually well mannered and pleasant. Her general behavior and alertness show the very constructive attention which her parents have given her. However, she does show tendencies often associated with an only child. She has a very active imagination and further, she expects attention whenever she wants it. She has an attractive appearance and is always clean and well-dressed. Ria is rather timid with her peers but feels at ease with adults. Her cultural background is upper middle class.

Ria is five years eight months chronologically, but somewhat more advanced intellectually. Part of this disparity can be attributed to the great amount of contact Ria has with the adult world. In addition, there are few children her age in the neighborhood; therefore, she has had to find her own amusement. She has been encouraged to "read" the many books in her home and already knows the letter names, but not their sounds.

Ria attended a private nursery school. She was well liked by the children there, but she seldom sought them out.

Results of the Scores Profile are as follows:

Listening Levels Measure	R
Pre-Reading Stages Inventory	3a, 3b, 3c, 2d, 2d
Sounding Status Index	11
Social Flexibilities Appraisal	IV

Other related information obtained on Ria states that her health is generally excellent, her speech is understandable and she uses a variety of words in her speech but does not often use complete sentences, and that she wants to learn to read.

Ria's Scores Profile and the other information obtained indicate that she apparently had no major pre-reading problems except with sounding and that she had achieved a Social Flexibility Level actually beyond that which a five year old child is expected to have achieved and which she needed to have achieved in order to begin to learn to read. In light of this information the Sound-Syntax Teaching Approach Emphasis was selected. In using this approach the parent began to teach Ria to read and at the same time help her develop valuable letter and letter combination sounding skills and a basic understanding of sentence structure.

In using the Sound-Syntax approach, the parent helps the child learn and relate or associate certain sounds with certain written symbols. She assumes the child will know the meaning of the word and that the word is already a part of his speaking and understanding vocabulary. The parent will also try to help the child construct sentences with the words he learns to read and see the function — the job of each word in the sentence (describing, naming, connecting, etc.)

When Ria's mother began using the First Phase Reader she taught the letters and words as suggested under Emphasis Key III in the Teaching Section of the reader. (If you will turn to the Gold section

133

at this time, you will note that every other page is used by you to teach your child the words and story on the facing page and that the section you are to use for a particular approach is designated by a corresponding key in the form of a Roman Numeral. Emphasis Key III is to be used with the Sound-Syntax Emphasis.)

Upon successfully completing the First Phase Reader, Ria's mother began the Second Phase Reader in the manner prescribed therein. After the reader had been successfully finished, she turned to the section entitled *Where to Go From Here* and obtained a number of suggested books for Ria.

You are ready, finally, to teach your child to read. You should, at this time, stop and congratulate yourself on your patience and meticulous labor. Since you have very carefully accomplished all of the tasks requested of you by this book, you deserve a rest and maybe a party, if you can talk anyone into it. So, after taking your extremely well earned break or fling, turn to the Gold section.

Chapter Five

Step IV

The First Phase Reader

INTRODUCTION

Upon reading this introduction and then leafing through the pages of the First Phase Reader, you will discover that the most difficult part is behind you. The main thing you need to do now is to follow the outline given you for each page of the reader.

This outline, called the Teaching Section, is on the facing page of each reader page and consists of two parts. The first part of each Teaching Section page in the First Phase Reader consists of recommendations for specific teaching emphases and is entitled Teaching Approach Emphasis Key. Here, you are to use the particular techniques given for the specific emphasis you are utilizing with your child. The second, labeled General Procedures, is common to all teaching emphases and is intended to gradually lead you and your child into the balanced reading approach you will use in the Second Phase Reader. (This is also the approach your child will use later in school and throughout the rest of his life.)

You will note that the Teaching Approach Emphasis Key section is comprised of three separate divisions, each prefaced by a Roman numeral. Roman numeral I corresponds to Memory Unit Form, numeral II to Sound Syntax, and III to Visual Motor Touch. In every case, when using this section, you will work only with the numeral corresponding to the Teaching Approach Emphasis you have selected for your child. (You will recall that if your are using the Voice-Impress-Look Along, you will not be using the First Phase Reader.)

There is not a recommended time limit for each story. Do not progress until your child has mastered the story and you feel he understands both content and reading skills. It is stressed that you are to follow the outline given for each page. The free space around each text page is for your own remarks, ideas, and notes so that you may learn how to better help your child. Be sure to always use the illustration on each page for purposes of discussion.

You will begin with the First Phase Reader on the next page. Before you start however, you should sit down with your child and tell him that you and he are going to share a book. Furthermore, it is a book that will teach him to read, if he will pay close attention and do what you ask.

Emphasize that this part of the book belongs to him as well as you and that you are going to play teacher and he, student. Motivate him by leafing through the First and Second Phase Readers with him, stopping to comment on the various drawings when he expresses an interest in them. You should not however, permit him to use the book by himself. Again, stress that it is a book for the both of you to use together.

When you and he are ready to begin, turn to the page labeled, "The First Phase Reader, Warmwood and Company" and discuss the drawing. You might discuss it in terms of the characters (you may read him their names) and what he thinks they (the characters) will do. Then turn to the following pages and begin teaching.

136

First Phase Reader Section

WARMWOOD
and
COMPANY

Spot

Eeka

P

Warmwood

Ritz

J

Teaching Approach Emphasis Key

>Be certain to use only one . . . the one you selected as the most appropriate and summarized on the Individualized Generic History-Observation Form.

I. (Memory Unit Form)

>Use Exercise Models 1 and 2, then the next day use the General Procedures.

II. (Sound Syntax)

>Use Exercise Models 1 and 2, alternating them for the next two weeks for thirty minutes each day, five days a week. Then for the third week úse Exercise Model 3. At the beginning of the fourth week, (or later, if your child has experienced difficulty) use Exercise Model 4 with the facing page in this reader. The next day, use the General Procedures part of this page.

III. (Visual-Motor-Touch)

>Use Exercise Models 1 through 5, alternating them every five minutes for the next five twenty-five minute teaching sessions; then use the General Procedures portion for this page.

General Procedures

>Use the following to discuss the opposite page with your child.

>Tell him this is "Warmwood House."
>Color "Warmwood" if you want.
>This house has a name. What name is "Warmwood House"?
>Ask him to say the words after you. "Warmwood House".
>Can you spell your name?
>Can you spell the name of this house?

>What other words begin with "W"?
>Think of another word that ends with "ouse".

>Read the page out loud.
>Ask your child to make up a sentence using the word "house".

138

Warmwood House

Teaching Approach Emphasis Key

Be certain to use the appropriate one.

I.   (Memory Unit Form)

Use Exercise Model 3 by working with shapes of various kinds of houses.

II.   (Sound Syntax)

Review Exercise Models 1, 2, and 3. Use Exercise Models 4 and 5 before going to the General Procedures part. (Remember to refer to Exercise Model 15 for the sounding key.)

III.   (Visual-Motor-Touch)

Use Exercise Models 5, 6, and 7, alternating each every ten mintues for the next five thirty minute teaching sessions. After accomplishing this, use the General Procedures portion to teach the reading page.

General Procedures

Use all of the following to discuss the facing page with your child:

Ask him what "Warmwood" means.
Ask him to read the page aloud.
Ask him to point to "warm" in "Warmwood."

Is "Warmwood" large or small?
Do not teach him the words up in the picture.
Merely read them to him.

Explain why capital letters begin the line of words, by saying that the letter of the first word is sometimes changed and is always made larger to tell us that we are starting a new line or idea. Discuss this with him.

This is warmwood warm

Warm Warmwood House

Teaching Approach Emphasis Key

Be certain to use the correct emphasis as designated by its numeral.

I.   Use the Exercise Model 4 pattern to present the two new words on this page and to review "warmwood", "warm", and "house".

II.   Use the Exercise Model 6 pattern to review "warm", "warmwood" and "house" and Exercise Models 4 and 5 to introduce the new words "Eeka" and "mouse".

III.   Using Exercise Model 8 as your pattern, teach and review the individual letters in the words "warmwood", "warm", "house", "Eeka", and "mouse." Then, for the next five thirty minute teaching sessions, introduce the rest of the letters in their lower case (non-capitalized) form according to procedures outlined in Exercise Model 8. (Use Exercise Model 10 to introduce the capital "E".) When you have finished this, (your child need not have learned the letters, you are merely beginning to familiarize him with them) go to the General Procedures portion.

General Procedures

Use this with your child.

What is Eeka?
Can Eeka fly?
Why can't Eeka fly?
Have you ever seen a mouse?
Did the mouse look like Eeka?

Ask him to read the page out loud.
Can you think of another word that rhymes with mouse?
What do many people live in?

Note: Throughout the First Phase Reader use the drawings to discuss each page and for purposes of motivation. Before doing anything, you and he first look at the drawing on each page as you come to it.

Eeka Mouse

Teaching Approach Emphasis Key

Be certain to use the correct numeral with your child.

I.   Use the Exercise Model 4 pattern to introduce "creep".

II.   Review the letter names and the sounds he has learned by using Exercise Models 1, 2, and 3.

III.   For the next ten thirty minute teaching sessions, alternate Exercise Model 8 (giving it about twenty minutes each time) with any one of the first seven Exercise Models. Then introduce the new word "creep", using procedures outlined in Exercise Model 9. After doing this, go to the General Procedures section.

Note: Throughout the rest of the First Phase Reader, *use only the emphasis numeral* you selected in the first parts of this book before using the General Procedures. Do not move from one emphasis to another. Stay with the same emphasis throughout. If you do not experience success with an emphasis, wait until you are advised to switch.

General Procedures

Use all of these procedures in discussing the opposite page.

How does Eeka move?
Can warmwood creep?
Can you creep? Try to creep. Creep around the room.

What does the word creep sound like? (beep, steep)
Ask him to read the page aloud.

Do not teach the sentence up in the picture. Read it to your child.

Ask him to draw Eeka in if he wants.

Note: Through out the remainder of the First Phase Reader, use all of the items under General Procedures for each page, after you have done the activites suggested by your particular Emphasis Key. Remember, whenever a question is given in General Procedures, ask it aloud to your child.

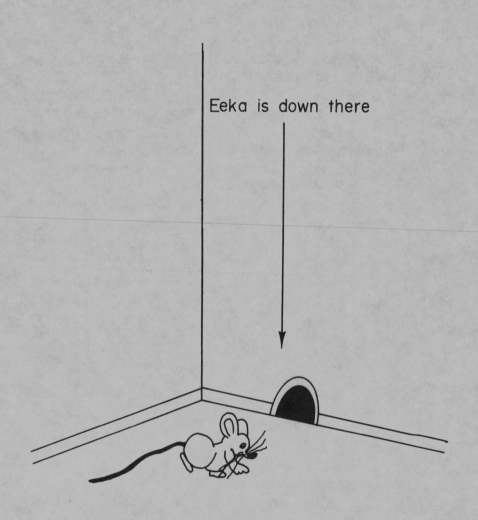

Eeka is down there

Creep Eeka Mouse.

Teaching Approach Emphasis Key

I.   Introduce all of the letters and words on this page by using Exercise Model 5 as a pattern.

II.   Introduce all the letters and words on this page by using Exercise Model 5. Then, for the next four teaching sessions, (or longer if needed) work with Exercise Models 9 and then 10. When he seems to have a general grasp of the short vowel sounds use the General Procedures part on this page.

III.   For the next ten thirty minute teaching sessions, alternate Exercise Models 8, 9, and 10 activites, taking approximately ten minutes for each of the three exercises every teaching session. (By this time your child should have two sets of twenty-six index cards; one set of small case and one set of capital letter cards.) Then, before going to the General Procedures portion, introduce all of the letters and words on the facing page by using procedures outlined in Exercise Models 9 and 12.

General Procedures

Use the following questions with your child:

Ask him to read the page out loud.
Ask him who is bigger?
Is J bigger than P?
Which one can move faster?
Do you think that J and P are friends?
Would you like to be friends with J and P?

Explain that the two ants are so small that their names are just letters.

Ask him if he knows anyone whose name is a letter or letters.
Tell him the S at the end of a word means more than one.
Ask him how many ants there are on the page.
Discuss the concept of "and" with him. (It connects)
Ask him to make up some sentences using "and".

J and P Ants

Teaching Approach Emphasis Key
I.   Read the page to him. Ask him to deal with the word "crawl" as suggested by Exercise Model 5.
II.   Before proceeding with this reader page, give at least two thirty minute teaching sessions to Exercise Model 11. When he seems to have a fair grasp of the long vowel sounds, introduce the word "crawl" and review "creep" and "house" by using Exercise Model 12.
III.   Go directly to General Procedures.

General Procedures
      Discuss the concept of the word "crawl".
      Have him act out this concept.
      Ask him to make up sentences using "crawl".
      Ask him to read this page out aloud.

      Note: Do not forget to use the drawing on each page as you come to it for purposes of discussion. Space around each drawing, on every page has purposely been provided so that you can use it to make notes as to how well he read the page, etc.

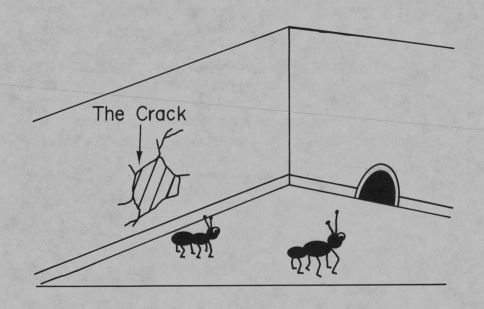

The Crack

Crawl J and P Ants.

Teaching Approach Emphasis Key

I.   Review these words, using techniques suggested in Exercise Model 5. Do not forget to use the General Procedures section after you use this emphasis.

II. Use Exercise Model 13 to review all of the words given to this point in the reader, using the techniques suggested in Exercise Model 12.

III. For the next five thirty minute teaching sessions, review Excercise Models 1 through 7, alternating one or more of them with fifteen minutes of instruction, using letters presented thus far in the reader. Use procedures outlined in Exercise Model 16. (If your child experiences difficulty with Exercise Model 16, give him exercises patterned on Exercise Models 6 and 7 until he can do Exercise Model 16.)

General Procedures

Ask him to read the page silently.

Ask him to read the page aloud.

Introduce the idea of direction. (back and forward) Say:

Can you crawl forward? Creep forward.

Can you crawl backward? Creep backward.

Can you crawl backward and forward at the same time?

Look at J and P and Eeka.

How are they moving? In what direction are they moving?

Creep and crawl.

Crawl and creep.

Teaching Approach Emphasis Key

I.   Introduce "see" to him, using Exercise Model 5 as your pattern. Ask him to read the page aloud to you. Then, give him part A of Exercise Model 6.

II.   Use Exercise Models 1 through 3 and 6 for the next two thirty minute teaching sessions. Introduce "see", using Exercise Model 12 as your pattern. Then, ask him to read the facing page silently and then aloud to you. Follow up this reading by using Exercise Model 4.

III.   Remember, always go to the General Procedures portion on every page after you have used the Emphasis Key activities. Using procedures outlined in Exercise Model 11, review all of the words he has learned to this point for the next five, thirty minute teaching sessions. Then, introduce the word "see", using procedures outlined in Exercise Models 11 and 12.

General Procedures

Review past concepts with him.

Ask him to read this page aloud to find out what Eeka is doing.

Be sure he knows these words.

See Eeka creep.

See J and P crawl.

Teaching Approach Emphasis Key

I.   Ask him to read the page silently to find out what Eeka and J and P are doing and then to read it out loud to you. Then, ask him to work with the words by drawing lines under them, as suggested by techniques given in Exercise Model 7. Pay particular attention to the word "go."

II. Introduce "go", using the technique suggested by Exercise Model 12.

III. Introduce "go" and review the words on the page using techniques outlined in Exercise Models 11 and 12. (Use Exercise Model 16 as a guide if necessary.)

General Procedures

Review "go" with him.

Ask him what it means to "go"?

Ask him to say a sentence using this new word.

Ask him to read the page aloud.

Ask him to draw J and P and Eeka here.

See J and P go.

See Eeka go.

Go J and P and Eeka.

Teaching Approach Emphasis Key

I. Use Exercise Models 5 and 7 patterns to introduce the words "so" and "long." Then, ask him to read the page to you.

II. Introduce the words "so" and "long" using techniques suggested by Exercise Model 4. Review the long and short vowel sounds using Exercise Models 10 and 11.

III. Using procedures given in Exercise Models 11 and 12, introduce the words "so" and "long". Review the words he has learned to this point by following procedures outlined in Exercise Model 13.

General Procedures

Use the following for discussing purposes with your child:

Why do we say "so long?"
What do we do when we say "so long?" (wave)
Where might J and P and Eeka be going?

Pick out the two words in "so long".
What does "long" mean?
Ask him to read the page aloud.

Note: Remember that you should not spend more than thirty minutes on any teaching session and you should have only one session per day.

So long J and P Ants.

So long Eeka Mouse.

Teaching Approach Emphasis Key

I.   Use Exercise Model 12 to introduce "abode". Review all of the words he has had up to this point by constructing an exercise similar to Exercise Model 4.

II.   Introduce the word "abode", using Exercise Model 12 as the pattern. Review the alphabet using Exercise Models 1 and 2.

III.   Teach the word "abode", using techniques outlined in Exercise Models 11 and 12.

General Procedures

Use the following for discussion purposes with your child.

Animals, like people, have homes or abodes.
What is your abode? (house, home, place)
Where might Eeka live?

Explain the apostrophe. Use a separate piece of paper.
The mark that looks like this ' in Eeka's name means that the abode belongs to Eeka.
Make up sentences using this mark to show that something belongs to one of your friends. (See Joe's pencil.)

Now let's look at Eeka's abode.

You may explain that Eeka prefers the word abode to home or house since she feels it sounds better, but because she had difficulty spelling it, she calls it her place.

What word rhymes with place? (race, face)
Spell place for him.

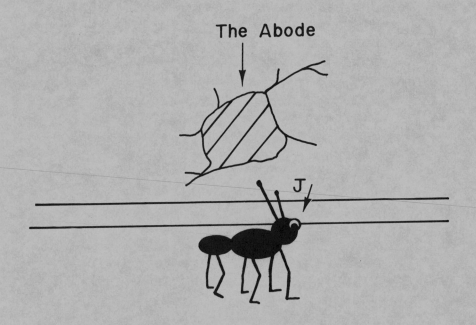

The Abode

Here is J.

Where is P?

See the abode, J?

Teaching Approach Emphasis Key

I.   Introduce the words "in", "lives", "is", "downstairs", and "where" using techniques suggested by Exercise Models 5 and 7.

II. Use Exercise Models 12 and 14 when applicable, to introduce "downstairs", "in", "where", "is", and "lives". Review the consonant sounds using Exercise Model 15.

III. Introduce the words "in", "lives", "is", "downstairs", and "where" according to the procedures outlined in Exercise Models 11 and 12.

General Procedures

Use the following for discussion purposes with your child:

What is the punctuation mark after the first sentence?
What is the punctuation mark after the second sentence?
Why do we use the question mark?
Why do we use the period?
Discuss the difference between asking and telling.
Have him practice asking and telling.
Ask him to read the page silently.

What is the first word of the question sentence?
What are other question words? (how, when, who)

Where is Eeka's abode?
Ask him to read the page aloud.

Note: Please recall that you are in no tremendous hurry to get through the First Phase Reader. Consequently, take as much time as your child needs for each reader page. Certainly, under no circumstances, could you hope to complete the activities given for your Emphasis Key and then the General Procedures *in less than one to two thirty minute teaching sessions.*

Ask him to draw Eeka's abode here.

Where is Eeka's abode?

Eeka lives in Warmwood.

Eeka lives downstairs.

Teaching Approach Emphasis Key
I.   Review the words on this page as suggested by Exercise Model 12. Ask him to read the page silently and then aloud to you.
II.   Use techniques suggested by Exercise Model 12 to review the words on this page.
III. Review the words learned to date by using the techniques suggested in Exercise Model 13.

General Procedures
(Do, regardless of your Emphasis Key after every page)

Ask him to tell you where J and P live.
Ask him to read the page to you.
Tell him that he may color the drawing if he wishes.

Note: Remember, always use the General Procedures portion in each Teaching Section after you have completed your Emphasis Key.

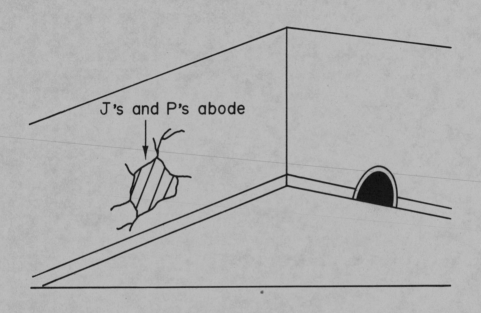

J and P's abode.

Teaching Approach Emphasis Key

I. Discuss the punctuation marks with him by asking which sentence gives the command. Introduce the words "here" and "the" by using the techniques suggested by Exercise Models 5 and 7.

II. Introduce the words "here" and "the", using Exercise Models 12 and 13 as the pattern. Discuss the meaning of the comma, (a pause) with your child.

III. Using procedures outlined in Exercise Models 11 and 12, introduce the words "here" and 'the".

General Procedures

Ask him to read the page silently to find what J is supposed to see.

Discuss the meaning of the word "command" with him.

Request that he now read the page aloud, paying attention to the comma as he reads.

Ask him to read the command sentence very loudly. (the last one)

Where are J and P?

Here are J and P.

See J and P crawl to the crack.

Emphasis Key

I.   Introduce the words "to" and "crack", using the pattern suggested by Exercise Model 12. Ask him what "to" means in the first two sentences.

II.   Introduce the words "to", and "crack", using procedures outlined in Exercise Model 12. Then ask him which words on the page begin with a "c" and which with a "t".

III.   Using the techniques given in Exercise Models 11 and 12, introduce the words "to" and "crack". Review Exercise Model 16 if necessary.

General Procedures

Ask him to read the page silently to find where J and P are going.

Explain to him that "downstairs" is a compound word. (a word made up of two separate words.)

After he has read this page silently and responded to your question, request him to read it aloud.

Ask him to color the crack.

Tell him to find the compound word and then to point out and pronounce the two separate words in it. ("downstairs")

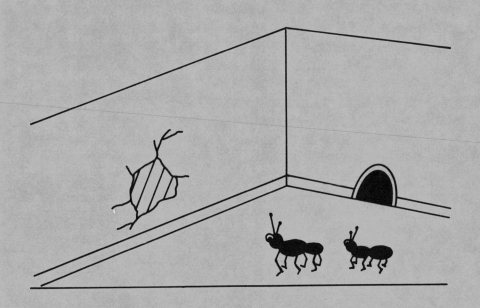

Crawl to the abode.

Crawl to the crack.

Crawl to the crack downstairs.

General Review

At this point, regardless of the Emphasis Key you are using, return to the Approach Emphasis description in the Blue Section which you selected at the outset and carefully reread its' description.

Please recall that you should use every illustration as a motivational tool. You are also reminded, that after using your specific Emphasis Key, to go to the General Procedures portion. *Do this regardless of your Emphasis Key.*

Please note that patience is a virtue possessed in abundance by all good teachers. You are a good teacher.

And finally, do not despair if you feel your child is not making adequate progress at this point. Stay with your teaching, using the Emphasis Key you started with. You will be advised later in this reader of the steps you should take if your child is not learning to read.

When you have finished rereading your teaching emphasis description, go to the next page in this reader.

Draw J, P, Eeka and Warmwood.

Emphasis Key

I.   Introduce the word "are", using the techniques suggested by Exercise Model 5. At this point, go back through the previous pages of the reader and print all of the different words on a sheet of lined paper. Be sure to print them carefully, by paying close attention to the letters that project above and below the lines. Then, give the paper to your child and ask him to draw lines under the words that overlap above and below the lines.

II.   Using procedures outlined by Exercise Model 12, introduce the word "are". Then review all of the words he has learned in this reader to date by using techniques suggested by Exercise Model 13.

III.   Introduce the word "are" according to the procedures given in Exercise Models 11 and 12. Review the old words on this page, using techniques suggested by Exercise Model 9.

General Procedures

(Always use this portion with every page after using your Emphasis Key.)

Discuss the illustration with your child by asking him what "J" and "P" are.

Then ask him to read the page aloud paying particularly close attention to the question mark and what it means.

Ask him to read the page aloud to you.

Here are J and P.

Here are J and P and Eeka.

Here are J and P and Eeka in Warmwood.

Emphasis Key

I. Introduce "enter" and "Spot" by using the techniques suggested by Exercise Model 5. Use Exercise Model 3 techniques to review different types of dogs.

II. Introduce "enter" and "Spot" by using techniques in Exercise Model 4.

III. Using techniques given in Exercise Models 11 and 12, introduce the words "enter" and "Spot".

General Procedures

Ask him what small word is in Spot. (pot)

Tell him he may color Spot if he wants.

Ask him to read the page silently to see if the words tell him about the illustration.

Ask him to read the page aloud.

SPOT

Enter Spot.

Emphasis Key
I.   Introduce "place", "under", and "couch" by giving him Exercise Model 5. Stress these words by having him do them first in the exercise.

II.   Use Exercise Models 5, 6, and 7 as a pattern for introducing the words "place", "under", and "couch". Both you and he closely examine the vowel sounds in the words and see if you can come to any conclusions regarding reasons for them being long or short. (In doing this, look at the ou and stress that the o and u together make their own special sound. Compare "couch" with "house".

III.   Use Exercise Models 11 and 12 to introduce the words "place", "under", and "couch". Using a number of the word cards, do Exercise Model 13.

General Procedures

Ask him to read the page silently to determine where Spot's place is located.

Ask him if any of the sentences are questions.

Have him read the page aloud being sure to use the voice inflection appropriate to the punctuation marks. (He should not raise his voice at the end of each sentence.)

Compare words such as "under" with "over", "above" with "below", "up" with "down".

Ask him to act out the differences in these words.

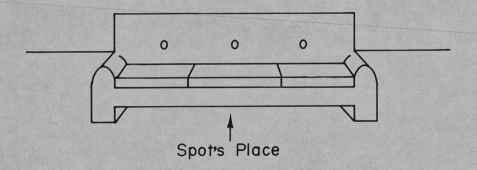

Spot's Place

Spot's place is here.

Spot lives in Warmwood.

Spot's place is under the couch.

Emphasis Key

I. Ask him to first read the page silently and then aloud for you. Introduce "whistling" by using techniques suggested by Exercise Model 6.

II. Ask him to read the page silently and then aloud. Then introduce "whistling" by using procedures outlined by Exercise Model 5. Discuss the "ing" ending, by saying it can control a word, so as to make it do something now.

III. Ask him to spell "whistling". Have him read the page silently and then aloud for you.

General Procedures

Can you think of a word which rhymes with couch? (grouch, ouch)

Ask him to make the second sentence into a question.

Is Spot whistling?

Ask him to again read the page aloud to you.

Note: From time to time, for purposes of review and variety, use some of the earlier Exercise Model procedures given for your particular Emphasis Key.

Spot is under the couch.

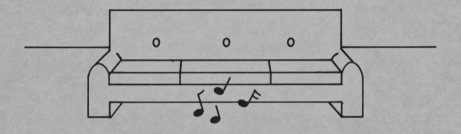

Spot is under the couch.

Spot is whistling.

Emphasis Key
  I.   Review the words on this page using techniques suggested by
       Exercise Model 5.
  II. Use Exercise Model 4 and then review the words on this page
       by using Exercise Model 12. At this point, you may want to
       explain to him, that the letter "r" controls the sound of
       vowels by changing them to a sound that is neither long or
       short.
  III. Repeat Exercise Model 13 using all of the word cards he has
       accumulated to date.

General Procedures
       Have him read the sentence silently and then aloud.
       Explain to him that the word "and" brings J and P and Spot
       together. So it is often called a connector.
       Read the sentence at the top of the page to him.
       Ask him to do what it says.

Draw J, P, Eeka and Spot here.

Where are J, P, Eeka and Spot?

Emphasis Key

I.   Introduce the words "come", "a", and "they" by using Exercise Models 4, 5, and 7 as your pattern. (You do not have to make drawings. Use the illustrations given.) Remember, always use the General Procedures part after you have used your Emphasis Key.

II.   Using procedures outlined in Exercise Models 4 and 12, introduce the words "come", "they", and "a". Use initial consonant substitution with "one" and see if he can give you some other words.

III.   Introduce "a", "come", and "they" by using the techniques given in Exercise Models 11 and 12.

General Procedures

Ask him to read the page silently.

Put your finger over the last letter in "warm".

What word did you make?

Ask him what sound does "m" make?

Ask him what does "they" mean?

Ask him if he owns anything that is warm?

Ask him to read the page aloud.

You print "lives" on a card and ask him to put his finger over the last letter and read the word.

Then ask him if it is the same word as a word on this page.

Spot is under the couch.

Eeka, Spot, J and P live in Warmwood.

Warmwood is a warm house.

Here they come.

Here come Eeka, J and P.

Emphasis Key
I.   Introduce "it", "holds", and "big" by using techniques suggested by Model 11.

II.   Using procedures outlined by Exercise Model 4 introduce, "it", "holds", and "big". Ask your child to give you the sound the letter "i" makes in "it". Ask him if "i" is a long, short or a special vowel sound. See if he can give you any other words beginning with "i" as it sounds in "it".

III.   Introduce the words "it", "holds", and "big" according to the techniques given in Exercise Models 11 and 12.

General Procedures
Ask your child to read this page first silently and then aloud to see if the words tell why "Warmwood" is warm.

Ask him if he believes this house is big enough to hold the story characters he has met thus far.

Note: A reminder that you should always use the General Procedures portion for each reader page after finishing with your specific Emphasis Key.

Warmwood is a big house.

It holds Spot and Eeka.

It holds J and P.

It is a big abode.

Emphasis Key
I. Introduce "friendly", and "your" by constructing an exercise similar to Exercise Model 6.
II. Introduce "friends", "friendly", and "your" by using techniques suggested by Exercise Models 5 and 6. Explain that the "ly" is an ending and that in this case the final "y" has the long "e" sound.
III. Teach the new words "friends", "friendly", and "your" according to the techniques outlined in Exercise Models 11 and 12.

General Procedures
Ask him what words rhyme with "place"? (race, lace, trace)
Ask him to read the page silently to see if it tells where Spot, J, P, and Eeka are.
Request him to read the page aloud and to change the last sentence to read as a question.

Draw Spot, Eeka, J and P and Warmwood.

Spot, Eeka, J and P are friends.

Warmwood is a friendly place.

Your house is a friendly place.

Spot, Eeka, J and P are your friends.

Emphasis Key

I. Review words on this page by constructing an exercise patterned after Exercise Models 5, 7, and 8.

II. Review words on this page utilizing procedures outlined by Exercise Models 2, 6, and 7.

III. Review the story section "Enter Spot" by using techniques given in Exercise Model 15.

General Procedures

Tell him the two sentences on this page begin with the same word.

Ask him what that word is.

Ask your child to read the page, first silently and then aloud.

Ask him to do what the sentence at the top tells him to do.

Note: If, at this point you and your child do not feel adequate progress has been made because he is not learning to read at all, please refer to the blue section and the Teaching Approach Emphasis you have been using to determine what you are to do now. If you are told to try a different Approach Emphasis, *other than the Voice Impress-Look Along,* go back to the first page of this reader and begin again using this new emphasis. If you get this far again, and he still is not making progress, forget about this reader for awhile and use the Voice-Impress-Look Along Teaching Approach Emphasis.

Draw   your   house   here.

Is   your   house   warm?

Is your house friendly?

Emphasis Key

   I.   Introduce the word "explorers" to your child by using techniques suggested by Exercise Models 5, 6, 7 and 12.

   II.   Using Exercise Model 12 as your pattern, introduce the word "explorers". Discuss "explorers" in terms of the "r" controlled vowel . . . a special vowel sound. Review final "e" words already learned that make the medial vowel long. (the abode).

   III. Teach the word "explorers" by using Exercise Models 11 and 12 as your pattern.

General Procedures

     Read the sentence to your child.

     Ask him to read the page aloud to you.

Say: We want to see what happens in this story.

       (Give the child a reason for wanting to read this. Encourage him to wonder and speculate on what will happen.)

Say: What does "explore" mean?

Say: What word have you already learned which ends in "er"? (under)

       Spell "explorers" for your child.

       Ask him what the "s" on the end of a word can mean. (more then one)

       Tell him this is not always true however.

       Review "lives" with him to show that this is not always true.

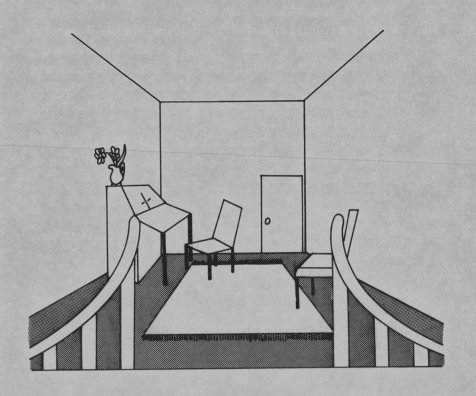

The Explorers

Emphasis Key

I. Introduce the words, "from", "good", "day", "out", "said", "spoke", and "came" by patterning exercises after Exercise Models 5, 8, and 14.

II. Using procedures outlined by Exercise Models 7 and 12, introduce "from", "good", "day", "came", "out", "said", and "spoke". Explain that "spoke" begins with a consonant blend and then review Exercise Model 14. Stress that the "ou" in "out" is a special word blend with each letter acting together to make a new sound.

III. Teach the new words "from", "good", "day", "out", "said", "spoke", and "came" by using procedures given in Exercise Models 11 and 12.

General Procedures

Say: Notice the *quotation marks*. They set off what the characters are saying.

Who is talking in the first sentence?

Who is talking in the third sentence?

You take one part and your child the other.

You might be Spot and he can be Eeka. You can also be the "narrator" by reading the "in-between words."

Note: You might like to do this often on other pages to be sure that your child understands why the quotation marks are placed where they are and who is doing the talking. You might point out the comma between the conversation and the narration. Remember, this calls for a pause.

"Come out, Spot," said J, P and Eeka.

Spot came out from under the couch.

"Good day, J, P and Eeka," spoke Spot.

Emphasis Key
I.   Introduce the words "asked", "we", "want", "what", and "attic" by constructing exercises patterned after Exercise Models 5, 15, and 16.

II.   Introduce the words "asked", "we", "want", "what", and "attic" by using procedures outlined in Exercise Model 12. Review the vowel sounds in these new words with him.

III.   Present the new words "asked", "we", "want", "what", and "attic" by using techniques given in Exercise Models 11 and 12.

General Procedures

Print the word explorers on a card and then ask him to cover the last two letters with his finger. If he does not know the resultant word, pronounce it for him.

Ask him what Eeka tells Spot to do on this page?

Ask him to read the page silently to find out what Eeka says. Point out to your child that action words tell what the characters *do*.

Ask him to read the page aloud.

"Come, Spot, we want to explore," spoke Eeka.

"Explore what?" asked Spot.

"We want to explore the attic," J and P said.

Emphasis Key

I. Introduce "Ritz", "ok", "but", "with", "yes", "you", "dark", and "mysterious" by patterning exercises after Models 5, 14 and 17.

II. Using Exercise Models 4 and 12 as your pattern, introduce "Ritz", "ok", "but", "with", "mysterious", "yes", "you", and "dark". Use Exercise Model 14 to review "Spot".

III. Teach the new words "Ritz", "ok", "but", "with", "mysterious", "yes", "you", and "dark" by using Exercise Models 11 and 12 as your pattern.

General Procedures

Ask him to read the page silently to find out which sentences J, P, and Eeka say.

Ask him to read the page aloud to discuss which sentences Spot does not say.

See if he can make some sentences beginning with "It is".

Encourage him to make other sentences to add to Spot's conversation.

Draw Spot, Eeka, J and P here.

"You want to explore the attic?" Spot asked.

"Yes, yes, yes," they said.

"It is dark and mysterious, " Spot said.

"O. K., but I want Ritz to go with us," spoke
Spot.

195

Emphasis Key

I.   Introduce the new words "this", and "hello" by using suggestions recommended by Exercise Models 5 and 9.

II.   Using Exercise Model 12 as your pattern, introduce the words "this" and "hello".

III.   Introduce the new words "this" and "hello" by using procedures outlined by Exercise Model 14. (If he is not ready for this exercise at this time; use Exercise Models 11 and 12 as a substitute for Exercise Model 14 until such time as he is able to do the exercise.

General Procedures

Read the following questions to your child:

Who is this?
What do you think Ritz might like to do?

Ask him to read the page aloud to you.

This is Ritz.

Hello Ritz.

General Review

By this time, you and your child should have settled into a familiar routine with regard to the new word introduction. Throughout the remainder of this reader, the new words will be introduced in the same general fashion with some minor variation.

Even though your child appears to be progressing nicely, using the word introduction techniques suggested by his specific Emphasis Key, you should review some of the first Exercise Models he was exposed to from time to time.

If your child is making satisfactory progress at this point, encourage him to read other easy materials on his own. But please, let him read them independently. Do not make a reading lesson from every reading-material he is interested in.

Please go to the next page in the reader.

Draw Ritz, Spot, Eeka, J and P.

Emphasis Key
 I. Teach the words "print", "name", "key", and "yelled" by using the techniques suggested by Exercise Model 13.
 II. Introduce the words "print", "name", "key", and "yelled" by using procedures outlined in Exercise Model 12.
 III. Use Exercise Model 14 as your pattern to present the new words "print", "name", "key", and "yelled".

General Procedures
  Ask him to read the page silently to find out if this is anything he should do.
  Help him print in his own name on the page.
  Ask him to read the page aloud to determine who speaks the last sentence on the page.

"Hey Ritz," yelled Spot.

"Good day, Spot," spoke Ritz.

"Good day, _____ "
said Spot and Ritz.

Print your name up here.

Emphasis Key
  I.   Teach the words "will", "please", "I", and "us" by using Exercise Models 6 and 13 as the patterns.
 II.   Teach "will", "please", "I", and "us" by using techniques suggested by Exercise Model 12.
III.   Use Exercise Model 14 as your pattern to teach the new words "will", "please", "I", and "us".

General Procedures
 Ask him to read the page silently to find out what Ritz says.
 Ask him to give you some other words we use to describe an attic.
 Ask him if he would like to explore an attic.
 Ask him to read the page aloud.
 Ask him to define the word "attic".
 Give help if he needs it.

"Ritz, J, P, Eeka and I want to explore the attic," said Spot.

"Will you come with us?"

"It is dark and mysterious," said Ritz.

"Please," said Spot.

"OK, I will come with you," spoke Ritz.

Emphasis Key

   I.   Introduce the word "exploring" by using Exercise Model 5 as the pattern. Review the old words on this page by using techniques suggested by Exercise Models 6 and 14 after he has read the page silently.

   II.   Teach the word "exploring", using Exercise Model 12 as the pattern. Review the "ing" ending by asking him what words he can make by placing different single letters in front of "ing".

   III.   Introduce "exploring" by using the procedures outlined in Exercise Model 14. Then ask him to read the page silently to find out what Ritz intends to do.

General Procedures

Say to him that Ritz was talking on this page and the author did not use quotation marks. Ask him to read the page silently to answer why.

(Because here, only Ritz is talking. He is talking to himself, and not to anyone in particular.)

Point out the *exclamation mark* in the third sentence. Then say: This mark (!) shows excitement. It is used after sentences that show more feeling than usual. Sometimes we say these sentences a little louder than sentences that end with a period.

(Give some examples)

Candy is so good for you!
The car is going very fast!

Ask the child to make some sentences that might have exclamation marks after them.
Ask him to read the page aloud paying close attention to the exclamation mark.

204

I will go with Spot.

I want to go exploring.

They want to explore the attic with me!

So long, Warmwood downstairs.

Emphasis Key
I. Ask him to do Exercise Models 10 and 11. Introduce "begins" by using procedures outlined by Exercise Model 12.
II. Review the words he has learned to date by using Model 13 as your pattern. Introduce "begins", using Exercise Model 12.
III. Review the story section "The Explorers", by using Exercise Model 13 procedures in written form. Dramatize this same story section by using the procedures given in Exercise Model 15. Then, introduce the new word "begins", using Exercise Model 11 as your pattern.

General Procedures
Ask him who is going exploring?
Ask him to tell you where the attic is located in "Warmwood."
Have him read the page aloud to you.

The Exploring Begins

Emphasis Key

I.   Introduce the words "shadow", "get", "darker", "vases", "tables", and "chairs" by using techniques suggested by Exercise Models 5, 6, and 13.

II.   Teach the word "darker" as "dark-er". Explain that the "er" ending makes whatever word it is added to, become more. For instance, you might say to him that the "er" ending usually changes the word to something more, eg., see if he can give you some additional examples. Introduce the words "tables", "vases", and "get" by using procedures outlined in Exercise Models 4 and 12 and 14 (for chairs and shadows.)

III.   Introduce "shadows", "get", "darker", "vases", "tables", and "chairs" by using Exercise Model 14 as your pattern.

General Procedures

(Always use this portion after you have used your specific Emphasis Key).

Ask him to read the page aloud and while reading, to add some other things that they might have seen.

Discuss the words "up-stairs" and "down-stairs" with your child.

Ritz and Spot go upstairs.

It begins to get darker.

They see shadows of vases, chairs and tables.

Emphasis Key

I.   Go over the word "me" by comparing it with "I". Use Exercise Model 5 as a pattern to teach this word and the word "yipes".

II.   Teach "me" and "yipes" by using procedures outlined in Exercise Model 12.

III.   Introduce the words "me" and "yipes" by using techniques given in Exercise Models 11 and 12.

General Procedures

(This is a good page for the child to act out. You might have him take turns reading different parts.)

Ask him to read it silently.

Point to the first word on this page. ("yipes")

Ask him when we use that word.

Ask him to make some sentences using that word as if he were excited.

Point out the words "hello" and "good day". When do we use those words?

Ask him to think of some other words to use as greetings?

Ask him to read the page aloud.

"Yipes, here are J and P," spoke Ritz.

"Hello Ritz," said J and P.

"Good day," said Ritz.

"Come to the attic with me."

Emphasis Key
I.   Introduce the words "hi", "am", "going", and "all" and review the old words on this page by using the suggestions in Model Exercises 6, 13, and 17.
II. Teach "hi", "am", "going", and "all" and review the previously learned words on this page by using Exercise Model 12 as a pattern. See how many words he can make by substituting different beginning letters to "all".
III. Use Exercise Model 14 as your pattern to teach the words "hi", "am", "going", and "all". Then review this story section, "The Exploring Begins", by using the procedures outlined in Exercise Model 13 (use it in written form) and Exercise Model 15.

General Procedures
Ask him to read the page silently to find out what J and P say.
Tell him to color Eeka gray.
Ask him to read the sentence that asks a question out loud.

"Eek, a mouse," yelled Ritz.

"Hi Ritz," said Eeka.

"Are you going exploring?" asked Eeka.

"Yes, will you come?" asked Ritz.

"Yes, yes, I will come," said Eeka.

"We will all go exploring," said J and P.

Emphasis Key
    I.   Review the words on this page using techniques suggested by Exercise Models 4 and 12.
   II.   Review the words on this page according to procedures outlined in Exercise Model 4.
  III.   Go directly to the General Procedures.

General Procedures
    Ask him to read the page silently to see if the illustration is explained.
    Ask him to read the page aloud to you.

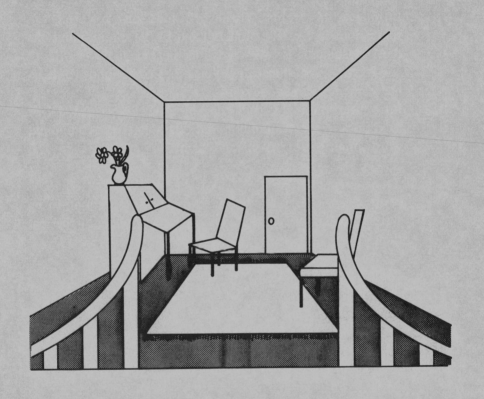

They Get to the Attic

Emphasis Key

I. Teach him the new words "flashlight" and "on" by using techniques suggested in Exercise Model 5. Review the old words on this page by using techniques suggested by Exercise Model 16.

II. Introduce the words "flashlight" and "on" by using the suggestions in Exercise Models 4 and 12. Be sure to point out that "flashlight" is two words together, made up of "flash" and "light". Ask him to tell you other compound words he has learned. (Warmwood, downstairs, upstairs).

III. Introduce "flashlight" and "on" by using Exercise Model 14 as your pattern. Remind him that "flashlight" is a compound word comprised of "flash" and "light".

General Procedures

(You might ask your child some nonsense questions to be sure he is thinking about these words as symbols of the real things they represent.)

Are shadows bright?

Ask him to color this page.

Ask him to read this page silently to find out how Spot may feel.

Ask him to read the page aloud to find out who turned the flashlight on.

Warmwood is warm and big.

The shadows get darker.

Ritz gets the flashlight on.

Spot begins to whistle.

Emphasis Key

I. Teach the words "eyes", "bigger", "louder", "faster" by using Exercise Model 12 as a pattern.

Introduce "eyes" by using Exercise Model 4 as your pattern.

II. Teach "bigger", "louder", and "faster" by printing the words without the "er" ending on separate cards and then asking him to sound each one out. Remind him about the special "ou" sound. When he has learned these words, simply ask him to add the "er" ending to each.

III. Use Exercise Model 14 as the pattern to present the new words, "eyes", "bigger", "louder", and "faster".

General Procedures

Ask him to read the page silently to find out whose eyes get bigger.

Ask him what kind of voice he thinks Eeka might have?

Ask him what kind of voice he thinks Spot might have?

Ask him to read the page aloud.

Explain that "er" on the end of words can intensify or make the words more. For example, slower, faster, etc. But this is not always so.

The shadows get darker.

Eeka's eyes get bigger.

Spot whistles louder.

J and P crawl faster.

Emphasis Key
    I.   Introduce the words "door", "top", "outside", "stop", and "inside" as suggested by Exercise Model 5. Ask him to do Exercise Model 10.
    II.   Teach "inside" and "outside" as compound words. Introduce "top", then ask him to put an "s" in front of it for "stop". Teach "door" stressing the special "oo" vowel sound. Use Exercise Model 13 as a pattern for the teaching and review of these words.
    III. Introduce "door", "top", "inside", "outside", and "stop" by using Exercise Models 11 and 12 as the pattern.

General Procedures
    Ask him to read the page out loud to see where they stop.
    Ask him to color the door.
    Ask him if the attic is close to the bottom of the house.
    Ask him to read the page aloud to you.

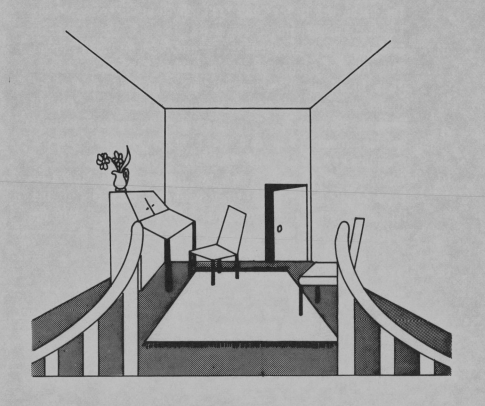

They come to the top.

They open the attic door.

It is dark inside.

They stop outside the door.

Emphasis Key
  I.   Teach the word "for" and "talk" by using Exercise Models 12 and 14 as patterns.
  II.   Introduce "for" and "talk". Ask him to blend the "f" sound with the "r" controlled vowel "o" as "or" to get "for". Then, blend the "t" sound and "al" as in "all" and the "k" sound to produce "talk." Explain that in many cases, the "l" controls the vowel "a" just as the "r" does to produce a special sound. (You can use Exercise Model 15 as the sounding key for the single consonant sounds.)
  III. Introduce "for" and "talk" by using Exercise Model 14 procedures. Review this story section, "They Get to the Attic" by using techniques given in Exercise Models 13 (in written form) and 15.

General Procedures
    Use the following to discuss the page with your child:

    What are our friends doing now?
    Have you ever stopped for a talk?
    Ask him to read the page out loud.
    Do you think that Eeka, Spot, Ritz, and J and P will find anything?

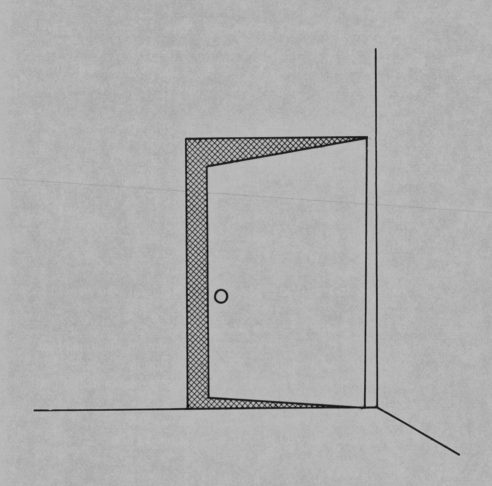

They stop for a talk.

Emphasis Key
- I. Introduce the words "anything", "let's", "cannot", "hear", "do", "say", and "pretty" by constructing exercises similar to Exercise Models 5, 12, and 16. Remind him that "anything" and "cannot" are compound words. Discuss these with him.
- II. Teach "any-thing" and "can-not" as compound words. Teach "let's", "hear", "do", "say" and "pretty" by using the procedures suggested in Exercise Model 12.
- III. Use Exercise Models 11 and 12 as the pattern to introduce "anything", "let's", "cannot", "hear", "do", "say" and "pretty". Remind him that "anything" and "cannot", are each made up of two separate words.

General Procedures

Ask him to read the page silently to find out who wanted to go on.

Have him to read the page orally.

Ask him if he has ever been in a dark and mysterious place. Discuss the apostrophe "s" as a contraction in this case.

It does not show a possession. The apostrophe indicates that a letter has been left out.

See if he can give you the letter. ("u" for "us".)

If he cannot give you the letter, explain it to him.

"Look J, P, Spot and Eeka. Let's go in," said Ritz.

"Stop whistling Spot, I cannot hear Ritz," spoke Eeka.

"It is pretty dark inside," said J and P.

"Do you want to go inside?" asked Ritz.

"Yes, let's go inside," said Eeka.

Spot did not say anything.

Emphasis Key
I.   Teach the words "just", "bone", "milk", "need", "first", "little", "scared", "hungry", "later", and "can" by using Exercise Models 6 and 16 as your patterns. Teach the word "scared" by discussing the word "look" and the ending "ed", meaning past tense.
II. Review Exercise Models 10, 11, and 15 and then let him work out the new words on his own. The new words are "just", "bone", "milk", "need", "first", "little", "scared", "hungry", "later", and "can."
III. Introduce the words "just", "bone", "milk", "need", "first", "little" "scared", "hungry", "later", and "can" by using procedures outlined in Exercise Model 14.

General Procedures
Ask him to silently read the page to find out who speaks last.
Ask him to read Spot's part aloud.
You read J and P's part.
Ask him if he thinks J and P would like milk.

"It is dark and mysterious in the attic," said Spot.

"I need a bone and milk first."

"Spot is a little scared," said J and P.

"I am not. I am just hungry," Spot said.

"You can get a bone and milk later," spoke Ritz.

"Yipes, OK," said Spot.

Emphasis Key

    I.   Use the techniques suggested by Exercise Models 5 and 6 to teach the new word "happening".

    II.   Teach "happening" as "happen-ing" by giving him the word so divided on a card. Let him sound out the individual letters, blend them together, and add the ending to produce the word.

    III.   Introduce "happening" by using Exercise Models 11 and 12 as the pattern. Review this story section, "They Stop For A Talk" by using the procedures outlined in Exercise Models 13 (oral form) and 15.

General Procedures

    Ask him to read the page aloud.

    Get him to speculate on what the happening could be.

The Happening

Emphasis Key

   I.   Introduce the words "moved", "over", "filled", "things", "boxes", "was", "crates", and "trunks" by using techniques suggested by Exercise Models 12 and 14. Ask him to read the page silently.

   II.   Teach the words "moved", "over", "filled", "things", "boxes", "was", "crates" and "trunks" by reviewing Exercise Models 14 and 15 and then letting him sound out the words on his own.

  III. Use the procedures outlined by Exercise Model 14 to teach "filled", "things", "boxes", "was", "moved", "over", "crates" and "trunks". Ask him if "things" is a familiar word to him. (He has previously learned the word "anything". Discuss this with him.)

General Procedures

    Use the following for discussion with your child.

    What was in the attic?
    How do you suppose Ritz and Eeka feel now?
    Ask him to read the page silently.
    Ask him why there are no quotation marks. (no one is speaking to anyone else in the story.)
    Have him read the story aloud.

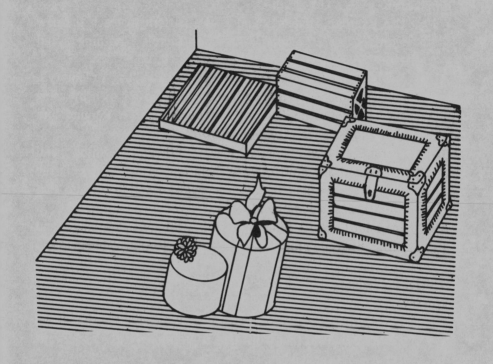

They opened the door and went inside.

Ritz's flashlight moved over the attic.

The attic was filled with things.

There were boxes and crates and trunks.

It was dark.

Emphasis Key

I.   Use Exercise Models 5 and 8 as a pattern to teach the new words "bag", "empty", "well", "there", "nothing", and "too". Ask him to do Exercise Model 10.

II.   See if he can work out the new words "bag", "empty", "well", "there", "nothing", and "too" on his own by using the techniques implicit in Exercise Model 12. Remind him that "nothing" is a compound word.

III.   Introduce "bag", "empty", "well", "there", "nothing", and "too" and ask him to work them out on his own using the techniques implicit in Exercise Model 12. Remind him that "nothing" is a compound word.

IV.   Introduce "bag", "empty", "well", "there", "nothing", and "too" by using procedures outlined by Exercise Model 14.

General Procedures:

You say:

Notice the word, "too". What does it mean in the sentences? Have we had another word that is pronounced the same way? How was it spelled? (to)

What did it mean? Give an example using the word, "too."

Give another example sentence using the word, "to."

These words are called *homonyms.* Homonyms are words that sound alike but have different meanings and are spelled differently.

Ask him to read the page silently to find out who saw the bag first.

Have him read it aloud to you.

"Look, you all, here is a big bag!" Ritz said.

"What is in the big bag?" Spot asked.

They all looked. It was empty.

"Well, time to go," said Spot.

"There is nothing here."

"Yes, time to go," said Eeka too.

Emphasis Key
I.   Introduce the words "another", "wait", "ran", "crept", "crawled", and "whistled" by constructing exercises similar to these given in Exercise Models 6 and 7. Ask him to do Exercise Model 8.
II. Teach the words "wait", "ran", "crept", "crawled", "another", and "whistled" by using procedures outlined in Exercise Model 12. Stress that "another" is a compound word that he can break down. Review endings which make words past tense.
III. Present "another", "wait", "ran", "crept", "crawled", and "whistled" by using techniques suggested by Exercise Model 14.

General Procedure
Ask him to read the page silently to find out who crept.

Say: Who found the other door first?
       What does "another" mean?

       Ask him to read the page out loud changing the words "crept" to "creep", "ran" to "run" and "crawled" to "crawl".
       Discuss how the meaning of the sentences are changed when this is done.

"Wait, look, here is another door!" Ritz said.

"Yipes, no, not another door," said Spot.

Ritz ran to the door.

Eeka crept to the door.

J and P crawled to the door.

Spot whistled at the door.

Emphasis Key
    I.   Use Exercise Models 12 and 15 as a pattern to teach the words "on", "but" and "happy".
    II.   Permit him to work out the words on this page on his own by asking him to blend individual letters sounds. (Do not read the words aloud to him first.) Stress that sometimes the final "y" makes the sound of the long "e". Review with him the fact that when the same two consonants appear side by side, only one of them is sounded.
    III.   Introduce "on", "but", and "happy" by using Exercise Models 11 and 12 as the pattern.

General Procedures
    Use the following questions to discuss this page:

    What does Ritz have in his hands?
    Color the flashlight blue and Spot white.
    Discuss "but" as a connecting word.
    Why do you suppose Spot does not look happy?
    Ask him to read the page silently and then aloud.

"Come on Spot," said Ritz.

"We want to look inside," spoke J and P.

"I want to go inside the door," said Eeka.

"OK," said Spot. But he did not look too happy.

Emphasis Key
  I.   Review the word "happen" and teach "bigger" by using
       procedures outlined in Exercise Model 5. Review the "ing"
       ending by using the above procedures, telling him it means
       something in the present as contrasted with an ending such as
       "ed" which can mean something in the past. Then, have him
       do Exercise Model 8 before going to General Procedures.
  II. Review the "er" ending with him and get him to work out
       the word "bigger" on his own. Identify this word for him by
       pointing to it, but not saying it aloud.
       Go directly to General Procedures.

General Procedures
Say: What other things might be in this picture?
       What do you think the bigger happening is?
       Are you sure they will find something?
       What does "happening" mean?
       Ask him to read the page aloud.

The Bigger Happening

Emphasis Key

I. Introduce the words "now", "hurry", and "pulled" by using procedures outlined by Exercise Models 6 and 12.

II. Ask him to work out the word "now", "hurry" and "pulled" on his own by telling him to find the new words on the page and then reading them. If necessary, review the special vowel sound of "ow", the long "e" sound of the final "y" in hurry, the "ed" ending and the rule that only one consonant sound is given for a pair of the same consonants in a word. (In this case, the "ll".)

III. Teach "now", "hurry", and "pulled" by using techniques suggested by Exercise Model 14.

General Procedures

Say: Did they go inside?

Why are there exclamation marks in the first two lines?

Can you imitate the characters going inside?

Which one do you think will get there first?

Which one will get there last? Why?

Can you make some more sentences with the word, "hurry"?

Ask him to read the page silently.

Should your sentences end with exclamation marks? Why or why not?

"Hurry Spot! Come Eeka, J and P," said Ritz.

"We will look inside this door now."

They went to the door and pulled it open.

Emphasis Key
I. Review the words on this page through techniques suggested by Exercise Models 5 and 14.
II. Review Exercise Models 8, 10, 11, and 15, if necessary, with your child.
III. Review the words on this page by using Exercise Models 11 and 12 as your pattern.

General Procedures
Ask him to read the page silently to see what was in the room.
Have him read the sentence aloud that ends in an exclamation mark.

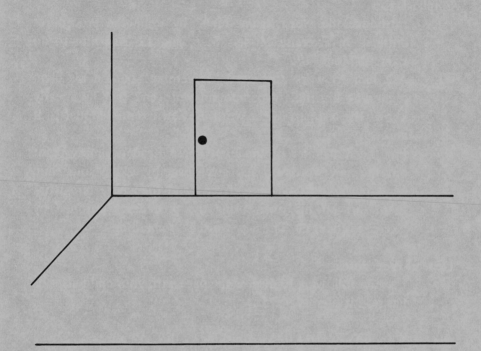

It was dark.

It was mysterious.

The room was empty.

"Let's go downstairs," Spot said.

"OK," they all said.

Emphasis Key
- I.   Introduce the word "something" by using the procedures outlined in Exercise Models 5, 6, and 12. Ask him to do Exercise Model 17.
- II.   Ask him to work the word "something" out on his own, reminding him it is a compound word and that he already knows the last part of the word. Review Exercise Model 14 if necessary.
- III.   For the remainder of the First Phase Reader, simply point out the new words on any given page by asking your child what new words he sees, if any, and then have him work them out on his own, using the procedures outlined by Exercise Model 14. The new word is "something".

General Procedures

Use the following to discuss the page with your child after he has read it silently.

Who did not want to see anything?
Who whistled?
What did Eeka say it was?
Ask him to read only the conversation aloud while you read the narration.
Review the (ed) ending with him. (whistle ed)

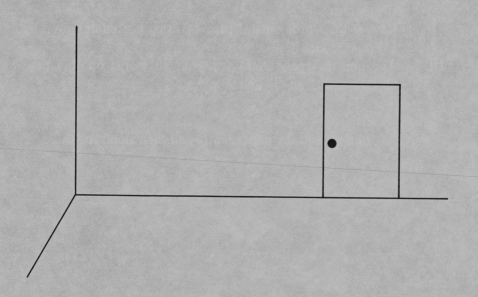

"Wait, I see something," said Ritz.

"You do not see anything," spoke Spot.

"Yes, I see it too," said J and P.

"It is another door," said Eeka.

Spot whistled.

Emphasis Key

I.   Review the words on this page by using Exercise Model 5 as the pattern.

II.   Review the words on this page by using procedures given by Exercise Model 12.

III.   Ask him to spell aloud for you, all words on this page beginning with an "l" and a "w".

General Procedures

    Ask him to read the page silently and then aloud to you.

Draw them all going to the door.

"Look," said Ritz. "Let's go inside."

Ritz ran to the door.

Eeka crept to the door.

J and P crawled to the door.

Spot walked to the door.

Emphasis Key

I.   Introduce the words "green", "glass" and "jar" by using the techniques suggested in Exercise Model 12.

II.   Ask him to independently work out the words "green", "glass", and "jar" after you have silently pointed to each one in turn and stated that it is a new word. Remind him of the "r" controlled vowel if necessary.

III.   Introduce "green", "glass", and "jar" by saying that these are new words on the page and then pointing to each of them in turn, but not pronouncing them aloud. Then, ask him to work them out on his own, using the procedures outlined in Exercise Model 14. If he experiences difficulty in doing this independently, give him help.

General Procedures

Say: What did they find?

Ask him to read this page silently to find out.
Ask him to read the page aloud to you and to be sure and finish the last sentence with the word he has printed in.
Discuss the word he used to complete the sentence.

Ritz pulled open the door and they all went inside.

The room was dark.

The room was mysterious.

There was something in the room.

It was a big, green glass jar filled with —————— .

Print what you think it is here.

Emphasis Key

I.   Go directly to General Procedures for this page.

II.   Go directly to General Procedures for this page.

III. Go directly to General Procedures for this page.

General Procedures

Ask him to read the page aloud and then use the following for discussion:

How do you know that it is time to stop playing or exploring or whatever?

(By seeing it get dark, by hearing your stomach growl because it's supper time.)

How many story characters are there in this picture?

Who do you suppose "they" can be?

Color this picture with dark colors.

"It is a good green jar _____ ," said Spot.

"Yes it looks fine," said J and P.

Do we need a green jar of _____ ?"
Eeka asked.

"No, but I am hungry," Spot said.

"I feel hungry too," said Eeka.

Emphasis Key
  I.   Introduce the words "good", "fine", "need", and "feel"
       according to procedures outlined in Exercise Models 5 and
       16.
  II. Ask him to work out the words "good", "fine", "need" and
       "feel" on his own after you silently point them out to him.
       Review the special vowel sound of "oo" if necessary.
  III. Point to each of the new words. Ask him to spell them aloud.
       Then, ask him to work them out independently. The new
       words are "good", "fine", "need", and "feel".

General Procedures
       Ask him to read the page silently.

Say: Do you get hungry at the end of the day?

       Review the "s" ending on "looks".
       (Does it make it more than one or what?)

They look happy.

They are waiting.

They are looking.

Emphasis Key
   I.   Go directly to the General Procedures section.
   II.   Go directly to the General Procedures section.
   III. Ask him to spell aloud all words on the page which begin with an "s".

General Procedures
   We say "so long" or "good-bye" to our friends every day and usually we are not sad to go. Sometimes we are sad to leave our friends. Can you remember times when you had to say "so long" to someone and you were sad?

   Remind him that the "s" without the apostrophe can mean more than one.
   Ask him to read the page out loud.

Draw all of them going downstairs.

"Let's go downstairs," said Ritz.

"So long," they all said and they went downstairs.

Emphasis Key

I.   Ask him to read the page silently first and then aloud, after you have used procedures outlined in Exercise Model 12 to introduce the words "her", "room", and "called".

II.   Ask him to work out the words "her", "room", and "called" on his own, after you have pointed them out to him. If necessary, remind him of the special "oo" word sound, the "ed" ending and the "er" ending sound. Ask him to read the page silently.

III.   Ask him to read the page silently, stopping at any word he does not know and spelling it aloud. As he spells each word aloud, ask him to independently work it out by using procedures outlined by Exercise Model 14. The new words are, "her", "room", and "called".

General Procedures

Use the following for discussion purposes.

Do you think Ritz was happy to go back to his room?
Do you think he wanted to go to Eeka's abode or to J and P's crack?

Do you think someone is waiting for Eeka at home?
Who is waiting for Eeka?

J and P crawled to the crack they called home.

Eeka crept to her abode.

Spot went to his couch.

Ritz went to his room.

Emphasis Key

I. Teach the word "company" by using the procedures suggested in Exercise Model 12.

II. Ask him to work out the word "company" on his own, after you silently point it out to him. Remind him, if necessary, of the final "y" having a long "e" sound.

III. Teach the word "company" to him by helping him pronounce it if necessary.

General Procedures

Ask him to read the page silently and use the following for discussion purposes.

Now, everyone is downstairs. How do you think they feel?
When you are in your room, and it's dark outside, how do you feel?
Do you think everyone feels safe when they are home?
What is Warmwood House happy about?
Ask him to read the page aloud.

Draw   Warmwood   here.

All   of   Warmwood's   Company   are   in   the
places   they   live.

Warmwood   House   is   happy.

Are   you   happy?

Draw   a   happy   looking   Warmwood.

The   end

Emphasis Key

Regardless of the emphasis you have been using, follow the General Procedures outlined below.

General Procedures

Review the entire First Phase Reader with your child for the next week or so to see that he has mastered the vocabulary and understands what he has read.

To review; ask him a question he must answer by reading a page; let him read it silently; then, ask him the question again; let him answer; give him another question for that same page and have him read it orally to you and then, ask him to give you the answer. Follow this procedure for each page.

Chapter Six

Step V

The Second Phase Reader

INTRODUCTION

By this time, your child should have acquired sufficient skill to permit him to easily reread the First Phase Reader. In general, if he has mastered the Reader's vocabulary and understands what the words tell him, he is ready for the Second Phase Reader. (Of course, you have obtained a good idea of his skill from the way he performed on the First Phase Reader review.)

Now you are ready to begin the Second Phase Reader. You will recall it was stated that this reader does not include a separate and distinct Emphasis Key section. The reason for this is now that your child has achieved a certain degree of reading proficiency based on a specific mode of learning, he needs to obtain a more balanced and comprehensive way to read.

261

Research in reading appears to indicate that a balanced approach to reading is the most efficient, once a certain degree of reading proficiency is attained. The balanced approach given in the teaching portion of the Second Phase Reader actually combines the critical elements of all the preceding Teaching Emphases into a unitary mode. Another reason for using the balanced approach in the Second Phase Reader is that there is at least a ninety per cent probability that this, or a very similar approach, will be used with your child when he begins school.

The format of the Second Phase Reader has been arranged so that the new vocabulary introduction can be made through a variety of approaches. The different approaches and other procedures you are to use with the Second Phase Reader are given in the Teaching Section provided for the stories.

For you and your child to derive maximum benefit from this Reader, it is suggested that you now carefully study the two Approach Emphasis descriptions given in the Blue section which you *did not* use with your child. You will need a full understanding of all three emphases (excluding the Voice Impress-Look Along) to teach from the Second Phase Reader.

You may find that it will be necessary to review early Exercise Models within a new Emphasis Key, with your child, before using the ones specified in this reader. If you find that this is necessary, spend four of five thirty minute sessions on them before proceeding.

You will note, as you proceed through the Second Phase Reader, that the Teaching Sections become more abbreviated and that the entire Reader is somewhat more brief than the first Reader. The reason for this is that the assumption has been made, that by now, you have become a more proficient teacher and your child an accomplished reader.

The primary goal of the Second Phase Reader is to give your child a balanced reading method and you, a general pattern to follow in teaching your child reading, which you and he can transfer to other reading materials suggested at the conclusion of the Second Phase Reader.

262

Second Phase Reader Section

Each drawing relates to a story. Discuss these with your child by saying that you and he are going to begin a new and exciting group of stories.

TABLE OF CONTENTS

Questions   265

Dinosaur Joe   269

The Doll Who Ran Away   275

It   281

The Dot   287

My Story   295

You may use the Table of Contents to discuss the drawings on the
Second Phase Reader cover page. Go over all of the titles with your
child before going to the first selection.

**(Please, no more than one session per day
and more than five per week)**
Session I (30 minutes)

1. Read the poem entitled "Questions" to your child.

Before reading it, tell him what you plan to do and ask him
to listen carefully because you are going to ask him some
questions about it after you have finished.

2. Use the following questions for discussion purposes:

What is the title?
Who is talking in the poem? (a child)
Did you like the poem? (Why or why not)
Why did I call this a poem? (stress rhyming)

Session II (30 minutes)

1. Discuss the large question marks by asking him why they
   are there.
2. Ask him to make up a poem and dictate it so you can
   print it in the space provided.
3. Go to the Table of Contents and discuss same with your
   child. Tell him these are the stories he is going to read now
   that he has become a good reader.
4. Go to the Teaching Section for the first story, "Dinosaur
   Joe".

?

QUESTIONS

Sometimes in the morning

When it is still early day,

My toys seem to be asking,

What are we going to do today?

There are many places to explore

And too many things left undone.

There is so much to seek

That the world seems to shout,

Come, let's go, look around,

Why not take a peek.

?

First, downstairs to breakfast,

Then back to my room.

There I dress quickly,

While telling the world,

I'm coming, I'm coming soon.

?

?

Will I go outside and play,

Or will I stay in?

Should I go to the world,

Or should it come to me?

The answer is not important

It's the question which holds the key.

?

?

Now that you have heard a poem can you make up one? See if
you can. When you do, tell it to your teacher so that she can write it
down here.

My Poem

TEACHING SECTION
FOR
DINOSAUR JOE

Session I (approximately 30 minutes)

1. Go to the Table of Contents and read the title to him. Tell him this is the second story and then ask him to give you the page that begins the story.
2. Turn to the first page of the story. Ask him what the title is again and what he thinks may happen.
3. Introduce the words "he", "had", "three", "my", and "took" on the first page by using Exercise Model 12 in Memory Unit Form as your pattern. Discuss the illustration. Ask him to read the page silently to find out how many dinosaurs Joe has.
4. Introduce the words "invisibly", "sat", "closed" on the second page by using Exercise Model 4, Sound Syntax as your pattern. Discuss the illustration. (What is invisible?) Ask him to read the page silently and then aloud.

Session II (approximately 30 minutes)

1. Introduce the word "that" on the third page by using Exercise Models 11 and 12 of Visual-Motor-Touch as your pattern. Discuss the illustration. Review the apostrophe "s" with him.
2. Introduce the words "sit", "heard" and "his" by using techniques outlined by Exercise Model 12 in Memory Unit Form, after discussing the illustration on the fourth page.
3. Review the meaning of quotation marks with him. Ask him to draw the invisible dinosaur in the space provided.

Session III (approximately 30 minutes)

1. Introduce "why", "won't", "because", and "name" using procedures outlined in Sound Syntax Exercise Model 4 for the fifth page. Ask him to read the page silently. Review the meaning of the apostrophe when it indicates a missing letter. Ask him to read the page aloud.
2. Introduce "fix", "how" and "give" by using procedures given in Visual-Motor-Touch Model Exercise 9 for the sixth page of this story. Explain to him why the conversation is circled in the illustration, if necessary.

Session IV (30 minutes)

1. Introduce "wrong", "nowhere", "somewhere", and "yellow" according to techniques given in Memory Unit Form Model Exercise 5 for the seventh page of this story. Be certain to point out the compound words and the fact that the "w" in the word "wrong" is silent. Ask him to read the page silently and then aloud.
2. Have him read the eighth page first silently to determine how the dinosaur's eyes become visible, and then read the page aloud. Discuss the illustration.
3. Introduce "teeth" and "scared" by using techniques given in Sound Syntax Exercise Model 12 for the ninth story page. Ask him to read the page silently and then aloud.

Session V (30 minutes)

1. Discuss the illustration. Ask him to follow the directions given on the tenth page.
2. Introduce "company" and "put" on the tenth and eleventh story pages by using procedures outlined by Exercise Models 11 and 12 of Visual-Motor-Touch. Ask

him to read both pages silently and then aloud. Have him read and follow the directions given on the eleventh story page.

Session VI (30 minutes)

1. Introduce "instead" by using techniques suggested by Exercise Model 5, Memory Unit Form for the last page of this story. Ask him to read the last page silently to find how Dinosaur Joe got his name. Have him read the last page aloud.
2. Ask him to read the whole story silently.

Session VII (30 minutes)

1. Review the whole story according to procedures outlined by Exercise Model 12, Memory Unit Form.
2. Go to the Table of Contents for the second story and ask him to give you the title and the page it begins on. Using the title, ask him what he thinks the story will involve.

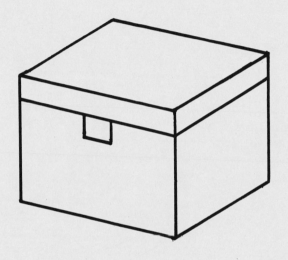

Dinosaur Joe

Joe had a big box.

He had three dinosaurs in the box.

"I am going to play with my dinosaurs," he said.

He opened the box and took out the three dinosaurs.

The Invisible Dinosaur.

He took out one big dinosaur.

He took out one small dinosaur.

He took out one invisible dinosaur.

He closed the box and sat down on the floor with his dinosaurs.

The invisible dinosaur is down there.

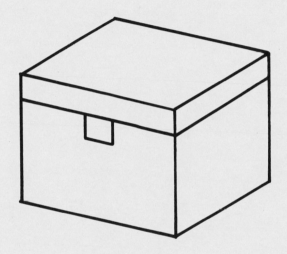

That is, he sat down on the floor with the big dinosaur and with the small dinosaur.

The invisible dinosaur sat on Joe's dinosaur box.

The invisible dinosaur says no.

Joe asked his invisible dinosaur to come over and sit down with him and the big dinosaur and the small dinosaur.

Joe heard the invisible dinosaur say no.

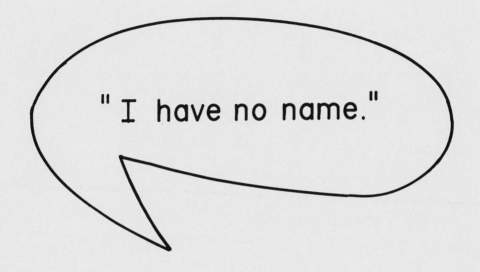

Why won't you come over and sit with us?" asked Joe.

"I will not come over and sit with you because I do not have a name," said the invisible dinosaur.

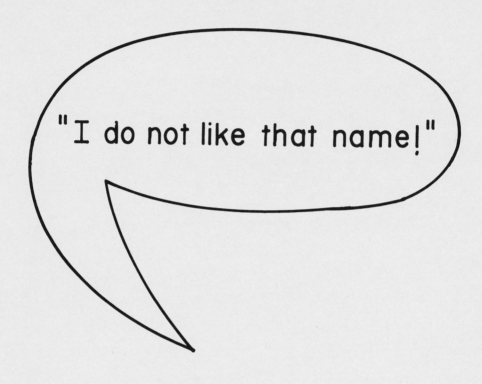

"Well, we can fix that," Joe said.

"How?" asked the invisible dinosaur.

"I will give you a name," Joe said.

How do you like the name, Nowhere?" asked Joe.

"No, no," said the invisible dinosaur.

"I do not like that name!"

"Well, what is wrong with that name?" Joe asked.

"Nowhere is wrong because I am somewhere," said the invisible dinosaur.

"OK," said Joe, "How do you like the name, Yellow Eyes?"

"I like it! I like it!" said the invisible dinosaur.

The invisible dinosaur's eyes became visible.

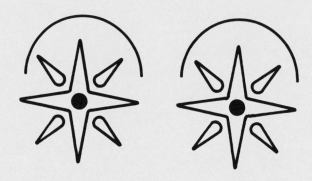

"Well then, Yellow Eyes it is," said Joe.

And with that two yellow eyes became visible.

"Yipes!" said Joe. "I can see two yellow eyes."

"No, only big yellow eyes," said Yellow Eyes.

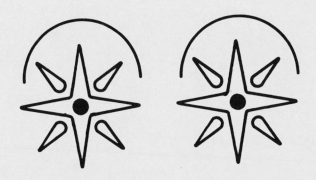

"You have big yellow eyes," Joe said.

"Do you have big yellow teeth too?" Joe asked, looking a little scared.

"No, only big yellow eyes," said Yellow Eyes.

Draw all three dinosaurs down there.

"Well, then we are friends," Joe said.

"Yes, we are good friends," said Yellow Eyes.

"Do you like the company of the big and small dinosaurs?" Joe asked.

"Yes, they are good friends too," said Yellow Eyes.

Draw Joe's box down there.

"I will put you in the box now," spoke Joe.

"OK, but when I want out, you let me out. I will not go from this room when I am not in the box," said Yellow Eyes.

"OK," said Joe and he put his dinosaurs in the box.

This is the end.

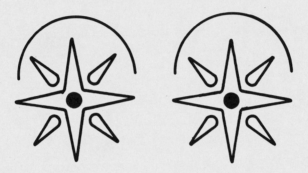

That is how Dinosaur Joe got a name.

He calls his invisible dinosaur Yellow Eyes now, instead of no name.

TEACHING SECTION
FOR
THE DOLL WHO RAN AWAY

Session I (30 minutes)

1. Return to the Table of Contents and ask your child to use it to turn to this story.
2. Discuss the title and illustration. Introduce the words "doll", "who", "ran", "away", "snowing", "cold", and "herself" by using Exercise Models 11 and 12 in the Sound Syntax as your pattern.
3. Ask him to read the page silently to find out what Kay decided to do. Have him read the page aloud.

Session II (30 minutes)

1. Discuss the illustration on the second story page. Introduce "many", "rares", "white", "black", "read", "brown", and "shall" by using Exercise Models 11 and 12 of the Visual-Motor-Touch as your pattern.
2. Review the apostrophe "s", here showing possession. Ask him to read the page silently and then discuss the phrase "many places and many races" to show color names. Have him read the page aloud.

Session III (30 minutes)

1. Discuss the illustration and ask your child to read the third story page silently to see how the text relates to the illustration. Ask him to read the page aloud, paying close attention to the way the words are combined to make sentences.
2. Ask him to give you the rhyming words.

3. See if he can reread it aloud, changing the words around so that there is no rhyming. (Help him if necessary)

Session IV (30 minutes)

1. Introduce "know", "snow", "Cleo", "high", "low", "could", and "find" by using Exercise Models 12 and 15, Memory Unit Form as your pattern.
2. Ask him to read this fourth story page silently to discover what Kay was looking for. Discuss the illustration and get him to make other comparisons of high and low.
3. Have him follow the directions given on the page.
4. Introduce the word "color", on the fifth page, using procedures outlined by Exercise Model 12, Memory Unit Form. Ask him to read the page silently to find out what Kay wants from her mother. Discuss the illustration and then ask him to do what the directions say.

Session V (30 minutes)

1. Introduce "seen", "just", "yesterday", and "close" according to techniques given in Exercise Model 2, Sound Syntax, for this sixth story page.
2. Discuss the illustrations after he has read the page silently to find out what was at the door. Ask him to read the story aloud.
3. Have him read this seventh story page silently to discover what was in the doll box. Discuss and have him follow the directions given in the illustration. Let him read the page aloud.

Session VI (30 minutes)

1. Tell him to read the entire story silently and carefully

because you are going to ask him some questions about it when he is finished.
2. When he has finished the silent reading, discuss the questions given on the last story page with him.

Session VII (30 minutes)

1. Complete item 2 in Session VI and then turn to the Table of Contents.
2. Ask him the title and page number of the next story.

It was snowing outside.

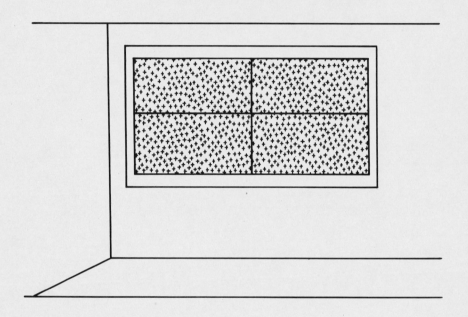

The Doll Who Ran Away!

It was snowing outside and it was cold.

Kay had nothing to do inside.

So, she went to her room.

When she got to her room she said to herself, "It is too cold to go outside and play."

"I have to stay inside, but what can I do?"

"I will get out my doll box," she said.

Kay's doll box.

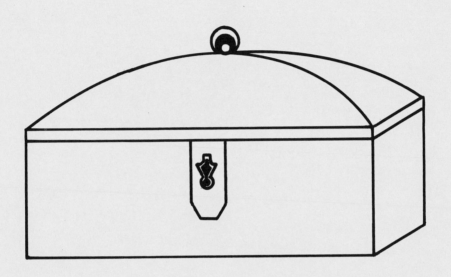

"I have many dolls," Kay said to herself.

"In the doll box I have dolls from many places and of many races.

I have white dolls and yellow dolls and red dolls and black dolls and brown dolls.

What doll shall I play with?"

I need a doll like the day.

I need a doll that likes the snow.

What doll is that to be?

What doll in snow will play?

What doll will I get from the box?

What doll, today, is for me?

Draw Kay up here looking high.

Draw Kay down here looking low.

I know, I know,

a doll for the snow.

I will get Cleo,

my doll Eskimo.

With that, Kay opened her

box and looked for Cleo

her doll Eskimo.

She looked high and she looked low

but she could not find her doll Eskimo.

Draw Cleo the doll Eskimo and color her brown.

Kay ran from her room to where her mother was.

"Mother, do you know where my Eskimo doll is?"
She asked.

"I do not know. What color is your doll Eskimo?"
Asked her mother.

"Well, she is not red or white or yellow or black,"
said Kay.

"She is brown," said Kay.

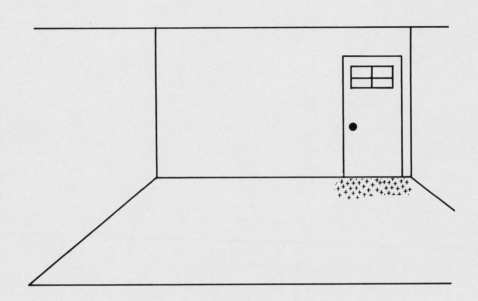

"I have not seen her, Kay" said Kay's mother.

Kay said, "Well, I put her inside the doll box yesterday. But she is not there now."

Just then, they heard the outside door open and close.

They ran to the door but no one was there.

There was just a little snow at the door.

Draw a little snow on Cleo.

Kay went to her room.

"Well, I will just play with my red doll," she
said to herself.

She went to the doll box and opened it.

"Yipes," she said.

There in the box was Cleo, her doll Eskimo.

And do you know that on Cleo, there seemed to
be a little snow.

Did Cleo go outside?

Did Kay look well for Cleo?

How did Cleo get snow on her?

Was it snow on Cleo?

Did the door open itself?

Did Kay play with the yellow doll?

Did Kay go outside?

Did Kay like Cleo?

What was Cleo?

This is the end of Kay's story.

TEACHING SECTION
FOR
IT

Session I (30 minutes)

1. Using the Table of Contents as a reference, ask your child to turn to this story.
2. Have him turn to the first page of the story and then discuss the title with him in terms of what he thinks "It" may be.
3. Introduce the word "corner" using Exercise Model 13 from Memory Unit Form. Discuss the illustration and then ask him to read the first page silently. Ask him to read the page aloud.
4. Introduce the words "knew" and "only" on the second story page by using Exercise Model 12 from Sound Syntax. Discuss the illustration with him and then ask him to read it silently and then aloud.

Session II (30 minutes)

1. Introduce the words "long" and "way" on the third and fourth story page by using Exercise Models 11 and 12 of Visual Motor Touch as your pattern.
2. Ask him to read both pages silently. Discuss the illustrations with him. Have him read the illustrations aloud.

Session III (30 minutes)

1. Introduce the words "stayed" and "about" from fifth, sixth, and seventh story pages by using Exercise Model 12 of Memory Unit Form as your pattern.

2. Discuss the three illustrations and then ask him to read the three pages silently to find out what "It" looks like.
3. Discuss this description and then ask him to read these same three pages aloud.

Session IV (30 minutes)

1. Introduce the words "began", "aha", "sure", "jumped", "later", "soon", and "smelled" as they occur on the eighth, ninth, and tenth story pages by using Exercise Models 11 and 12 of the Visual-Motor-Touch as your pattern.
2. Discuss the three drawings on these pages and then ask him to read the pages silently to tell you what "It" was. Ask him to read the three pages aloud to you.

Session V (30 minutes)

1. Teach the words "before" and "again" by using Exercise Model 12 of Memory Unit Form as your pattern.
2. Ask him to read this eleventh story page to you and then give you the answers.
3. Discuss the questions on the last story page. Allow him to answer them.

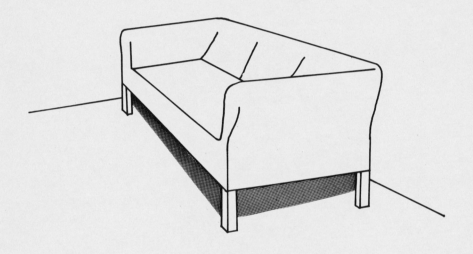

IT

Something was living under the couch in Joe's house. It lived in a corner where it was dark. It only came out when no one was in the room with It.

Only It knew it.

No one in the house knew It lived under the couch. Father

did not know it. Joe, Kay and Ritz did not know it. Only It

knew it and It was not talking.

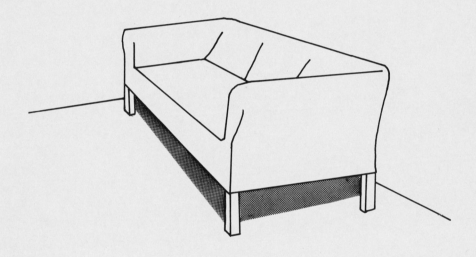

It had not lived in the house long. It had moved into the house

only yesterday. But It was looking for a way out today. It was just

too cold under the couch.

The sunshine bringing day.

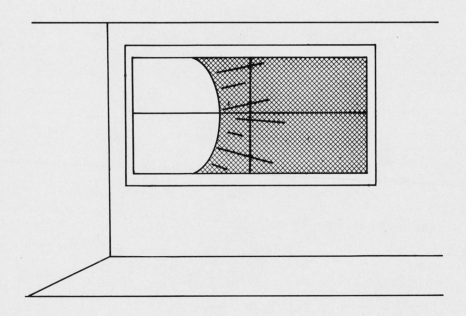

It knew it was morning. It could see vases, tables and chairs. It could see by creeping to the end of the couch and looking out. It could see Father, Mother, Joe, Kay and Ritz. But they could not see It.

This is under the couch.

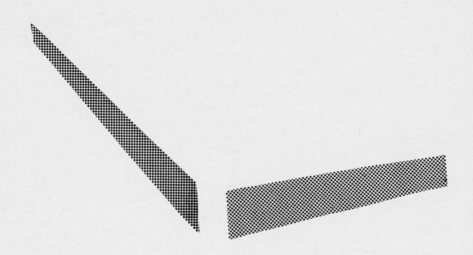

It wanted out. "If only I had not come in the open door yesterday," It said to itself. "If only I had stayed outside. I am so hungry."

"No one likes me."

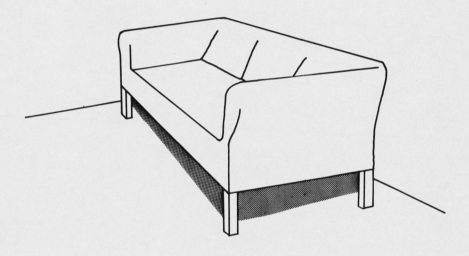

It crept back into the corner where it was dark. "No one likes me. No one likes green eyes. No one likes my white teeth," It said to itself.

Draw what you know about It here.

Do you know what It is? What do you know about It?

You know It can c _____ .   You know It is h_____ .

You know It has a long t_____ , green e_____ ,

and white t_____ .

Put in the missing words up there.

It began to creep out.

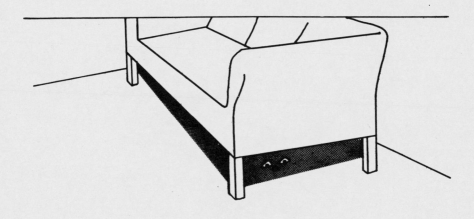

All the company went out of the room but Joe. Then It said,

"They have all gone. I will come out now." It did not know Joe

was in the room. It began to creep out.

Draw It jumping high into the air.

It crept out onto the open floor. "Aha," said Joe. "I was sure there was something under the couch." With that, It jumped high into the air and then ran back under the couch.

Joe ran out of the room. He came back a little later with some
milk and cat food. It was so hungry that It ran out when it
smelled the food. Soon Joe and It became good friends.

Draw It and Joe down there.

What was It? Do you know? You have all you need
to know to draw what It was. Can you do it? If you
are not sure, read the page before this one again.

Do you feel alone sometimes? How did It feel? Have you been cold? Do you have a cat? Is Joe a friendly boy? Do you like cats? Can you tell a story about a cat to your mother? Will you make it a good story?

The End

You are asked to use the following procedures for this and the last story in the Second Phase Reader: (1) Have him read each page silently while you read it over his shoulder or beforehand, (2) When he has finished a given page, discuss it with him by asking general questions concerning its content and then ask him to read it aloud to you. (3) Make sure that he does whatever a given page requests him to do. (4) He should be able to work out any unknown word he encounters in these last two stories on his own. (5) If he experiences difficulty in working out words, help him by using any of the Exercise Models with which he is familiar. (6) When you have finished a story, have him reread it silently and then orally to you. (7) Spend only about thirty minutes for each teaching lesson. (8) Make certain that he understands every story.

As he reads these last two stories, review and teach punctuation marks, special use of the apostrophe, paragraph indentation meaning, and literary meanings with him. Be certain to take your time. Do not let him flounder, help him when necessary.

The last story, "My Story", is intended as a culminating one. Most of the difficult words presented in the book are given again, in this story. In addition, full paragraph indentation is used with two or more paragraphs on each page.

In discussing paragraphing with your child, you will need to remind him that a sentence gives one idea while a paragraph gives a group of related ideas. That is, a paragraph consists of ideas that go with one another so that a better story can be told.

●

The Dot

This is a dot. It has a way of getting underfoot sometimes.

At other times the dot can be very handy.

There is no dot there. Where can it be?

Sometimes we forget to put the dot in when we print the

"i". When we do this, the "i" can look like an "l" or maybe a

"t". It is good to always put in the dot.

The dot's name is ——————— .

Let's pretend a little. Let's name the dot up there in the

drawing. I cannot think of a name. You think of a name for

the dot and put it in.

"I can think."

"I will not be good like a dot should."

What could happen if the dot moved by itself? What if the dot could think? What if the dot one day decided not to be good and not do what it should?

Let's pretend the dot just wants to play all of the time.

Now let's pretend that this dot is silly. Pretend that it wants to play all day and nothing else. See how silly the dot is in the drawing. It is just moving about and doing nothing.

Print your name for the dot here.

_____ Dot.

You must decide if the dot is a he or a she dot.

One day the little dot played outside for a long time. It had played so long that it was very tired. The little dot had not done any work at all! And the little dot had been needed for three things!

The little dot was wanted three times.

It was needed to end a line of print like this one.

It was wanted to dot an i.

It was needed to help make a polka dot dress.

As you can see from the drawing, the dot was very much needed. But it was out playing. So, other dots had to work overtime. They did not like this very much.

This is Big Dot hearing from the other dots about the little dot.

That is how Big Dot heard that the little dot was playing and not working. The other dots told him because they had to work too hard. They told Big Dot they were working so much that they were getting smaller. The other dots said if they did not get some rest they would just become nothing.

Big Dot was unhappy.

Big Dot again.

When Big Dot heard that the little dot was not being good and doing it's work he became very unhappy. He became so unhappy that he decided to do something about it right then.

Draw who Big Dot called here.

Do you know what that Big Dot did? He called his friend

the eraser! He asked the eraser to have a little talk with the

small dot. And you know what that could mean!

The Big Dot and the eraser.

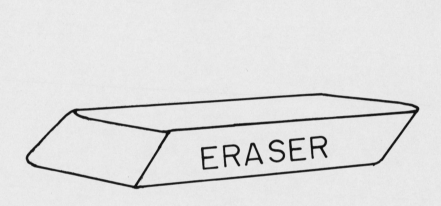

The eraser told Big Dot he would be happy to talk with the little dot. So the eraser went looking for it. But the little dot could not be found. The eraser looked high and low but he could not find the little dot.

Print in your name for the little dot down here.

_____ Dot went to work.

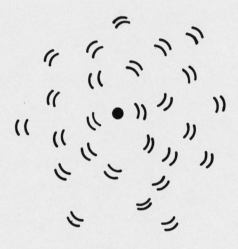

The eraser could not find the little dot because it was out

working. It had heard that the eraser was looking for it. The little

dot worked so hard that in one day it dotted three "i"'s, two polka

dot dresses and ended six lines of print.

What do you think happened to the little dot?

What do you think happened to the dot? Do you think
the eraser talked to the little dot? Do you think Big Dot
decided that the little dot would work now? What would you
do if you were Big Dot?

Talk over these things with your mother. Then make up a
new story about the little dot and Big Dot. Tell Mother the
story you made up when you can.

The End

My Story

Some time back, oh, two or three or four days ago, I saw some mysterious things. I want to tell you of these things so I have made up a story. Here is my story.

There is a street in a place I know called Green Street. There is a small house on Green Street colored yellow. Three people live in this house. They are Father, Mother, and Sam. Sam is a little boy.

You may be asking how I happened to know about the mysterious things I am going to tell you of. If there are only three people in the house, who am I? Well, I will tell you later. You can just guess for now.

Most of the rest of this story is about Sam. You can see what he looks like by thinking of a little boy like you or someone you know.

This will help you see Sam. He has big eyes and little feet. His hair is yellow and his hands are always moving. He likes to play but he does not like to work around the house.

Well, now to the mysterious things I want to tell you about. First, there was this thing that happened in the kitchen.

One day, while Sam's mother was in the kitchen, she said she had too much work to do. And there was a lot of work too. The floor was dirty. There were dirty dishes and the table had food on it.

Well, while Mother was saying this, Sam was in a room close by. You could tell he heard his mother because he looked up and sat very still while she was talking to herself.

Sam's mother went on to say to herself that she did not have time to work in the kitchen then. She had to go down the street and stop by a friend's house for some talk.

Before she left she asked Sam to be good and not to go out of the house while she was gone. Sam said that he would stay inside and play with his dog Spot. With that, Sam's mother went out of the door.

It was very still in the house for awhile after Mother left.

But then, I heard this loud yell and I saw something white go

by very, very fast! Then it became still again.

I did not think any more about it and went back to what I

was doing. But later, I heard something moving in the kitchen

so I went in to look. And do you know, the kitchen was

clean!

All of the dishes and the floor were clean. The table did not have any food on it. It was so clean that you could see yourself in it.

It was very mysterious. Sam's mother and father did not know what to think. You see, when she came home she was just as much in the dark as anyone. No one knew who or what could have cleaned up the kitchen so well and so fast.

Mother called Sam in and asked what could have happened. He just smiled and said that he was not sure. So Mother decided that it could not have been Sam because she knew he did not like to do that kind of work very much.

That was the first mysterious thing. After that there were many others. And, always, just before a mysterious thing happened, you would hear this yell and maybe see a white something go by very, very fast.

One day I overheard Sam's mother talking to him. She said, "Sam I have a lot of work to do in your room. I have to sweep the floor, put away your toys and make the bed. Will you help me later? I do not have time to work now because I have to go out."

Sam spoke, saying, "Yes, I will be happy to help you when you come back. I too, do not have time to work now. Spot wants me to play with him upstairs."

Now, there was one thing said in all of this talking that was very mysterious. Sam had said that Spot wanted to play with him upstairs. That was it! That was the mysterious thing! That was it! You see, the house does not have an upstairs!

When Sam's mother left, I went into his room to see what he was doing. But, he was not there! Where was he? Did he go with his mother? Then I heard something move under the bed.

I walked over to the bed and looked under it. No one heard me walk over and look under. What do you think was under the bed?

Yes, you are right. It was Sam. He was putting something white on. He did not see or hear me.

I walked out of his room and stopped by the door to look. In a little while Sam came out from under the bed dressed in a white sheet. He still did not see me.

Then he yelled, "I am Super Speedy, the Good." With that, moving so very fast you could hardly see him, he made his bed, put up his toys and swept the floor.

Now you know how all of the mysterious things took place. It had been Sam all of the time. He wanted to help his mother, but as Sam, he did not like that kind of work too well. So he became Super Speedy, the Good for a little while, just to help her. You see, Super Speedy, the Good did not mind doing housework sometimes.

That is my story and also the last story in this book. I said that I would tell you who I am before this story ended. Do you know? Can you guess. I am Sam's dog, Spot.

The End

CONGRATULATIONS– to both you and your child for this very significant reading-teaching achievement. The following chapter is intended to give suggestions for where to go from here.

Chapter Seven

Where to Now

INTRODUCTION

Now that your child has finished the Second Phase Reader successfully he is reading at the very least, a high first or low second grade level. His main task at this stage is to maintain this degree of reading proficiency while increasing his stock of concepts and number of reading words.

The idea here is not to push the child on to a higher reading level but to maintain and enrich the reading capabilities at the level he has attained. In addition, since your child has acquired a complement of word attack skills and so can unlock many new reading words on his own, you need not teach a detailed daily reading lesson to him.

In brief, what is being said is that you should not push a good thing too far. There is a danger of helping him acquire a negative attitude towards the act of reading if he is pushed or "taught" from every book he evidences an interest in. For this reason, it is suggested that you allow your child to read independently for the most part.

Therefore, when you and your child make the book selections from the listing provided on the following pages it should be done with the idea that he will read most of each book independently. Generally speaking, from now until he begins formal schooling, you should work with him in the manner suggested in the following paragraphs for no more than one or two thirty minute sessions per week. The sole exception to this principle would obtain if your child asked you to work with him on a more frequent basis.

When you do work with the child from this point on you are requested to observe the following general procedures: (1) From time to time (at most, twice per week or when asked by your child) check on his reading status by having him read a page silently and then aloud for the purpose of answering specific questions you have put to him concerning the page's content. This implies that you read the page beforehand, give him some questions, have him read it, ask him the same questions again, and then discuss his responses. (2) If he experiences difficulty in unlocking a given word, help him by selecting any of the Approach Emphases you want to use as a reference. (3) Discuss any story he wants to go over with you. (4) Make each session as informal and interesting as you possibly can by varying the story discussions and by including follow-up activities such as role playing, constructing, walks, etc.

The following is a listing of materials you may wish to use for reading selection purposes. It is not intended as a comprehensive or exclusive listing. There are many excellent reading materials on the market which are appropriate. If you decide to use materials not on this list the only cautions you need to observe are that they are interesting to your child and are not above a high first or low second grade level of reading difficulty.

Note that the materials listing is grouped according to publishers. Most of the books enumerated cost from one to three dollars.

Abingdon Press
201 Eighth Avenue, South
Nashville, Tennessee

Hector Goes to School, Ruth Liehers
You Know What? I Like Animals, Bernice Carlson.
An Elephant, Lorna Balian.
Benjamin, Irene Elmer
Smart Mr. Tim, Elizabeth Jarratt
Cubby's World, Story of a Baby Bear, Robbie Trent
What a Silly Thing to Do, Norah Snaaridge
900 Buckets of Paint, Edna Beckner
Three Boys and A Dog, Gina Bell
The Boy Who Could't Roar, Grace Berquist
All the Children of the World, Helen Doss
Friends Around the World, Helen Doss
Where I Live, Mary Sue White
Farm Girl, Grace Berquist
See Me Grow, Mary Sue White
Who Has Seen the Wind? Marion Conger
How Do You Travel? Miriam Schlein
Science, Science Everywhere, Ruth Weir

E. P. Dutton and Company, Inc.
201 Park Avenue, South
New York, New York 10003

Dinosaur Twins, Inez Hogan
Eager Beaver, Inez Hogan
Fox Twins, Inez Hogan
The Littlest Bear, Inez Hogan
Twin Colts, Inez Hogan
Frardy Cat, Inez Hogan

Farrar, Straus and Giroux
19 Union Square West
New York, New York 10003

Adventures of a Beagle, T. L. McCready, Jr.
The Magic Christmas Tree, Lee Kingman

E. M. Hale and Company
Eau Claire, Wisconsin 54701

Andy and the Lion, James Daugherty
The Big Snow, Berta and Elmer Hader
The Crooked Colt, C. W. Anderson
Deer in the Snow, Miriam Schlien
Mr. Charlie's Pet Shop, Edith Hurd
How the Animals Eat, Millicent Selsam
The Busiest Boy in Holland, Lisl Weil
Ramon Makes a Trade, Barbara Ritchie
Suzie and the Bude Doll, Patricia Ritchie
Johann's Magic Flute, Robert Oberreick
Rain in the Winds, L. Londen
Riding the Rails, Elizabeth Olds
Mr. Charlie's Farm, Edith and Clement Hurd
All Ready for Summer, Leone Adelson
Wind, Jeanne Bendick
Johnny Crow's Garden, Leslie Brooke

Harcourt, Brace and World, Inc.
757 3rd Avenue
New York, New York 10017

My Friend Charlie, James Flora
B is for Betsy, Carolyn Haywood
Here's Penny, Carolyn Haywood
Jenny and the Wonderful Jeep, Sally Scott

Alphonse, That Bearded One, Natalie Carlson
Did a Bear Just Walk There, Ann Rand and A. Brinbaum
The House That Jack Built, Antonio Frasconi
The Little Igloo, Lorraine and Jerrald Beim

G. P. Putnam's Sons
390 Murray Hill Parkway
East Rutherford, New Jersey 07073

Snippy and Snappy, Wanda Gag
Millions of Cats, Wanda Gag
John F. Kennedy, Patricia Martin
The Craziest Halloween, Ursala Von Hyspel
That New Baby, Peggy Mann
The Doll House Mystery, Flora Jacobs

Random House, School and Library Service, Inc.
457 Madison Avenue
New York, New York 10022

Go, Dog, Go!!, P. D. Eastman
The Whales Go By, Fred Phleger
Look out for Pirates, Iris Vinton
Cowboy Andy, Edna Chandler
You Will Go to the Moon, Mae and Ira Freeman
The Cat in the Hat, Dr. Seuss
Book of Laughs, Beenett Cerf

Steck-Vaughn Company
P. O. Box 2028
Austin, Texas 78767

Daffy, Adda Sharp
A Book of Tails, Anne Gray
A Book of Tongues, Anne Gray
All the Sounds We Hear, Lee Nelson

References

Adams, Fay and Lillian Gray and Dora Reese. *Teaching Children to Read.* New York: The Ronald Press Company, 1949.

Artley, A. Sterl. *Your Child Learns to Read.* New York: Scott, Foresman and Company, 1953.

Bond, Guy L. and Eva Bond. *Teaching the Child to Read.* New York: The Macmillan Company, 1944.

Botel, Morton. *How to Teach Reading.* Chicago: Follett Publishing Company, 1962.

Cordts, Anna D. *Phonics for the Reading Teacher.* New York: Holt, Rinehart and Winston, Inc., 1965.

Dawson, M. A. *Guiding Language Learning.* New York: World Book Company, 1957, 160-192.

Duker, Sam and Thomas P. Nally. *The Truth About Your Child's Reading.* New York: Crown Publishers, Inc., 1956.

Durkin, Delores. *Children Who Read Early.* New York: Teachers College Press, 1966.

Durrell, Donald D. *Improving Reading Instruction.* New York: Harcourt, Brace and World, Inc., 1956.

Durrell, Donald D. *Remarks on Teaching Reading.* Durham, North Carolina: Duke University Reading Conference, 1969.

Fernald, Grace M. *Remedial Techniques in Basic School Subjects.* New York: McGraw-Hill Book Company, Inc., 1943.

Gates, Arthur I. *New Methods in Primary Reading.* New York: Teachers College Publications, 1928.

Gray, William S. *On Their Own in Reading.* New York: Scott, Foresman and Company, 1948.

Gray, William S. *Recent Trends in Reading.* Chicago: The University of Chicago Press, 1939.

Hester, Kathleen B. *Teaching Every Child to Read.* New York: Harper and Brothers, Publishers, 1955.

Hildreth, Gertrude. *Teaching Reading.* New York: Henry Holt and Company, 1958.

Luria, A. R. *Human Brain and Psychological Processes.* Riverside, New Jersey: Basic Books, 1966.

Mergentime, Charlotte. *You and Your Child's Reading*. New York: Harcourt, Brace and World, Inc., 1963.

Money, John.*The Disabled Reader: Education of the Dyslexic Child*. Baltimore: John Hopkins Press, 1966.

Montessori, Maria. *The Montessori Method*. New York: Frederick Stokes Company, 1912.

Natchez, Gladys. *Children with Reading Problems — Classic and Contemporary Issues in Reading Disability*. New York: Basic Books, Inc., 1968.

Ravenette, A. T. *Dimensions of Reading Difficulty*. London: Pergamon Press, 1968.

Robinson, Helen M. *Why Pupils Fail in Reading*. Chicago: University of Chicago Press, 1946.

Scottish Council for Research in Education. *Studies in Reading XXVI,* Vol. I. London: University of London Press, 1948.

Smith, Donald, and Patricia Carrigan.*The Nature of Reading Disability*. New York: Harcourt, Brace and Company, 1959.

Smith, Nila B. *Reading Instruction for Today's Children*. New Jersey: Presentice-Hall, Inc., 1963.

Strickland, Ruth G. *The Language Arts in the Elementary School*. Boston: D. C. Health and Company, 1951.